THE
TINY BEE
THAT HOVERS
AT THE CENTER
OF THE
WORLD

DAVID **SEARCY**

FOR LARWILL

THE
TINY BEE
THAT HOVERS
AT THE CENTER
OF THE
WORLD

PART ONE

1

ABOUT SEVENTY MILES NORTH OF PHOENIX, NANCY (MY GIRLFRIEND then, eventually my wife) spots a highway sign for Arcosanti. Good Lord. I had no idea. I would have thought it too abstract for a highway sign. This way to the strangely pure yet vague accumulation of ideas toward what the future ought to look like made of sand, as it seemed to me (or sandy concrete, I suppose), back in the seventies when you'd hear about it now and then, get glimpses on the news, a Sunday feature on the visionary architect Paolo Soleri and his followers who, termite-like, appeared to form those weird utopian architectural notions out of desert. I can't see anything out there but scrubby desert. We are on our way to Flagstaff, to Lowell Observatory. That's where Percival Lowell glimpsed canals on Mars a hundred and twenty years ago. His great refracting telescope, still maintained in its dome, at the time was among the largest in the world, with a twenty-four-inch objective lens by Alvan Clark and Sons, whose achromatic optics are, to this day, unexcelled. There's a famous photograph of Lowell peering through it—suit and tie, his cap on backward, sitting in a simple wooden chair like a kitchen chair on a platform crankable into position along the rails of this contraption like a giant library ladder. Such an awkward and elaborate presentation of himself to the tiny eyepiece of this brontosaurian instrument angled down to him for all the world as if he were the object of inspection. As I guess he would eventually become.

We've left the highway. I have learned to trust her instincts with regard to these departures from the path. We take a long, descending dirt road toward a scatter of undistinguished structures and storage containers, old construction equipment imperfectly hidden behind the ragged yellow plastic slats woven into a chain-link fence. I'm not encouraged. But, descending a little farther to the parking lot, we see we're on the back side. Not the side for presentation. We're to struggle a bit. I see. Get past the stages of denial, disbelief to find ourselves at last arrived into the dreamy concrete future Paolo Soleri had in mind—and kept in mind, though it would seem in the minds of fewer and fewer believers all these years.

I can remember in the seventies really admiring those somehow virtuous cast-bronze bells from Arcosanti. People hung them up like prayer flags—souvenirs of our better selves. Our better future selves, I guess. My friend Tim Coursey had one hanging from a tree in his backyard. I liked the strain of its exoticism. Such a tiny, ordinary thing to be utopian, futuristic.

Look! A wind chime from the future! How can you tell? Well, first of all it's asymmetrical—a sign of freedom, spiritual progress, I should think. And then the uninterpretable abstract decoration. Though the blue-green oxidation might incline one to imagine great antiquity. There's always that ambivalence. The way exoticism doesn't care in which direction it departs the here and now. It's the departure that beguiles and mystifies us, I suppose. Yet it seemed clear that here was a little bell from the future in my friend's backyard. We'd hear it ring sometimes and think, Well here it comes. The future is approaching.

So, how strange to come upon that future now, descended into. Not approached across the endless nowhere I had always imagined—like a mirage, like something glimpsed out there in the middle of Ray Bradbury's Martian desert, where it's always seemed the future ought to be. But down a dirt road, past the junkyard. You descend into a recognition of it—still and always under construction. Oh yes—there's that concrete tower of round-fenestrated cubes. And yonder—now that I can see them; from the road I'd thought them Quonset huts—the arching ever-futuristic, open concrete barrel vaults and the concrete semi-hemispheres with their archaic/futuristic crests. All set, like the Acropolis (whose elevated prospect Arcosanti shares when viewed from the proper side, the valley side), among the tall, funereal cypresses, which seem to serve—ambivalent, perverse—a broadly classicizing, antiquating function, as if thus to make the future more conceivable, accessible, presented as another sort of Periclean Age and, in a way, a curious way in its eternal incompletion, as a ruin.

This is the parking lot to anyplace—apartment complex,

supermarket. Surely, I am thinking as we pass along the walk, this delicate notion will collapse upon approach. But maybe not. It blurs but holds. That strange ambivalence carries through, fills up the three-story concrete interior of the gaping-huge-round-windowed visitors' center and café, where I've sat down with Nancy and the best lasagna (vegetarian) I've ever had and feel myself, right off the bat, to have arrived at a sort of physical re-alization of that vague and inexplicably nostalgic sense of the future I received in contemplating certain science-fiction paper-back cover art in the 1960s. I declare this is the best place in the world. It's all summed up, it seems to me, in the ambivalence. The future and the past. I sense, somehow, that it's all worked out. The aspiration. Incompletion. The lasagna. It's lasagna from the future. Try some, Nancy. She declines but seems to under-stand. She notes the gentle shabbiness that hangs about the fu-ture. Finds it touching, even comforting to not be able to tell if it's construction or decay. To not quite know in which direction the arrow swings.

God, how I loved that gauzy science-fiction paperback cover art. At its very best it seemed to present a sense of strange-ness as a pure and separable quality—a condition to be attained, or perhaps reduced to, in the future. You would get this Yves Tanguy–like space but gone all atmospheric, all worn out. This hazy, dusty, sad uncertainty way out to a faint horizon where some marvelous futuristic apparition could be glimpsed beneath a pair of moons or a red, inflated sun. Sometimes that strange-ness out there seemed to be a city. And that's what would really capture me. Suggesting that one could gather oneself toward that idea somehow. That we might gather into the future—and we're talking wildly distant future here—into such rarefied and lonely concentrations of ourselves like fluff from cottonwood or something. Beautiful, accidental residue of us. That can't be longing that one feels. That makes no sense. What, then? It looks a lot like eighteenth- or nineteenth-century Romanticism, doesn't it. At first. Those lacy, asymmetrical spires within that shining crystal dome out there in the red light of the dying, setting sun at the edge of everything on the 1957 Crest Books paperback cover of *City at World's End* by Edmond Hamilton. I doubt I ever read it. But the cover is enough. Just look at that. That should be tugging those same heartstrings tugged by ruins in the sunset in some old Romantic landscape. Wouldn't you think? A twelve-year-old of course would not. Or would not know. Or would not care.

So, after lunch we take the tour into the waning afternoon of Paolo Soleri's great experiment in urban sprawl reversal and collective human efficiency. One has to nod politely at the official non-futurist line—a theoretical point of style. But come on, look. It's plain to see that it is the struggle toward the future that appeals, the visible gesture that stands out in the fading light—in which we sense ourselves suspended like those spacey-looking bells they've always cast right here and sold to pay the bills, to keep it going. It works out. It all comes down to the bells in a way.

Soleri started with the bells, our tour guide tells us. No one seems to know exactly when or how the impulse struck. But first ceramic bells—produced by casting liquid clay, or slip, into a mold dug into earth. Eventually bronze bells cast into silt on a similar principle. And then—all this quite early in his career—a conceptual leap: ground-casting of concrete architectural forms—like the dramatic cubes and domes and vaults and "apses" here assembled into a complex not much larger than a shopping mall yet clearly, monumentally expressive of his vision of a vastly greater "arcological" structure into which society's functions might be concentrated, gathered into a more benign and rational relation to the world.

Soleri's written thoughts (and one suspects that few were left unwritten) tend to take the form of grandiose pronouncements. There's a sense of a man beset by inspiration. Finger always in the air. Yet I imagine—I can't help but find it touching to imagine back there somewhere—an unformulated, undramatic, sudden, quiet insight into something like the future of us all, the misty science-fiction paperback-cover future of us, gathered out of the earth like bells. The will to love and kindness and efficiency cast in place and softly ringing in our ears.

The bells are everywhere. All sizes, mostly chemically weathered bronze and usually ringing in the breeze. The bronze ones cast into silt from the river, hung from chains resembling vertebrae or other skeletal fragments and their spare, schematic ornament drawn or pressed into the surface of the mold, retaining something of that sandiness, that silty friability—a quality of accidental order, of impermanence, like ruins glimpsed from altitude or doodles on the beach—or certain passages from Percival Lowell's sketches, for that matter. And that's the thing about the bells, I think. The future seems regretful—excavated, oxidized. And all this tintinnabulation somehow faintly elegiac.

Most of the concrete structures here are built of sections cast in molds dug into the ground. These airplane hangar–sized barrel vaults are made that way, each massive, curving panel poured into the earth and lifted out, craned into place. The inner surfaces are frescoed. Actual frescoes—fading, rusticating, spiky green-and-yellow abstract desert vegetation arcing up from both sides into a red-and-orange-striped sky toward delicate pendant circles along the top that look a bit like falling stars—all painted first upon the molded earth, the wet concrete then taking in the stain. We yell (a couple of us yell) don't touch it, when our tour guide (Dan, I think) suggests there might be plans to freshen it up, the fading colors. God, don't touch it. That's the point. You know? The struggle for the future is allowed to get confused, become abraded; needs to have a little wiggle room to vacillate, unground us, shake the whole idea of history up in order to depart it. Here, for example, go Minoan. As these frescoes readily do—those at the Bronze Age palace of Knossos have these colors, this same level of abstraction.

The uncertainty itself almost seems formalized, a theoretical consequence of the strain involved in trying to extract the future from the ground, from history, bits of each adhering. Look at how they've set the ground-cast concrete panels with the sandy side, the ground side, facing out. And all hand-poured. None of that gorgeous, perfectly finished, artful concrete that you see so much these days in modernist structures—almost showy in its service to simplicity. This concrete shows the gaps, uneven surfaces and edges, places here and there where the aggregate clumped up. It shows the haul and dump and slump of all that concrete poured into a pure but not quite fully formed (nor fully formable) idea. It's like they've gone from napkin sketch to concrete just like that.

Soleri seems to have thought that way about it. Keep it light, experimental—inconsistent, even. Keep that sense of process that obtains as a sort of principle—no matter that there's been no major construction in the last—what? Twenty years or maybe more. Or that the resident population of disciples, workers, artists has declined from a couple of hundred, I think he said, to maybe thirty-five. And now with the death of Soleri, who can say how it will go. Yet still, with uncertainty, ambivalence so deeply, philosophically built in, the end is not to be determined. It's the future, after all. You keep that napkin-sketch transparency that lets you see right through toward all imaginable outcomes. Do not tidy up. Keep all that old construction equipment. Keep that rusting yellow crane parked down the slope above the guest rooms—that long bank of concrete cells that faces away across the valley and the endless present moment. Where one goes to sit and listen, I imagine, to the elegiac ringing from above and contemplate the aspiration, incompletion of one's life. One's better self, our better, stranger selves out there somewhere perhaps.

A little curly-blond-haired boy of five or so is in our group. He's on a pretty loose leash. He ventures close to precipices, peers into the silt-filled bronze bell casting boxes. Now and then he'll amble up to Dan, our bearded, earnest guide, remove his thumb from his mouth as a scholar his pipe, to make an observation. It won't make much sense, of course. He's only speaking to be speaking. But each time, Dan halts his spiel, looks down without the slightest trace of condescension, and attempts to do his best. Each time, Dan waits for a signal from the kid that his response—his muttered struggle toward response—has been accepted. There's a fairly constant breeze, a wavelike tinkling of the smaller bells that hang in little clusters here and there. I want to translate for the child. As for some alien representative. I want to make my way into that silence, bow apologies and offer to interpret if I may—and to suggest that our guest was noting that your women are allowed to wander freely. Or that he sees no sign of cattle. And thus finds the constant sound of bells confusing. That the meaning of this place is not as clear as it should be in leading one to know how one should situate oneself within it. How the blue sky seems to shoot straight through some structures, then get dammed up, go all dark and thick and cold inside some others like these south-directed half domes, like so much of it half-finished, open, cupped as if half-listening. Half-expecting. What? An answering sound of bells from somewhere south across the valley? Of your cattle coming home? That is a way to speak of the very distant future, is it not? And here we smile, whoever this is and I, to signify that we've made a little joke, then bow and, placing our thumbs in our mouths, rejoin the others.

Do we feel our incompletion all the time? Do cows come home? We're always never really coming home—like pastoralists, I imagine. With their cattle. I imagine we must keep a Paleolithic sense of that within us still. That longing built too deeply in to ever lose. So, how agreeable, perhaps, to be a pastoralist. Just be that—have that longing right in front of you, continuously addressed. To be forever lost and found. To have that hazy, dusty promise of arrival always billowing around you. Here we are, oh here we are. Like the Fulani of the Sahel that Anna Badkhen—writer, reporter from the desperate parts of the world—has told me about, having traveled with them for a season. You are lost, of course, but always being found. Your home is always in the coming to it. Longing always lifting like the dawn. This understanding, I imagine further (never having gotten any closer to the region than the stories Anna's told me), having seeped into the mud that builds the villages and cities to maintain a sort of memory of this. You've seen those monumental mud-brick structures rising from the desert, as unlikely as if carved from ice. As if no sooner imagined, wildly imagined, than constructed on the spot, out of the substance of the spot, the dust and dirt. An entire city conceptually clear and simple as making camp, deciding where you are. No more substantial than a camp of newly plastered grass-mat huts if not attended, in effect rebuilt continuously. The Great Mosque of Djenné in Mali, for example, surely the highest expression of mud-brick architecture in the world (rebuilt completely from its thirteenth-century roots in 1907 under the French by native architects and workers), gets replastered every year with fresh adobe, lest infrequent rain penetrate the cracks and compromise the mud-brick structure underneath. I can't help thinking how those workmen (never women, for some reason) slapping mud up there on the wall must reacquire that sense of having just arrived. Must gain a monumental sense of that arrival, that eternal incompletion that the pastoralist derives upon arrival yet again and again and again. Oh, here we are. Here's what we do—a common memory of loss and rediscovery. Just like cattle coming home. Like Arcosanti, built by the bucketful, the handful and the basketful of mud.

There was for a while in the 1970s a curious fashion for

painted landscapes on the sides of vans and minibuses. Sometimes other subjects, but by far most common here were empty landscapes. Usually desert. Everyone, it seemed, who had a van would have to have a desert painted on it. Auto insurers introduced a special category. Running down the list one time with an agent, I remember being asked, "How big is your mural?" For a moment I had no idea at all what he could mean. But, coming to understand, I felt the urge to lie, that here was something rather sensitive, beyond mechanical matters. Having to do with generosity of spirit, maybe. Vision, grace, expansiveness, or something. What had happened? When did all this come about? It was as if a special insight had been granted. Someone, somewhere on a car lot maybe, overcome among the blind, unpurposed rows of recreational vehicles. Standing, squinting with the salesman in the empty afternoon. Oh, there is something missing, surely, in the glare from all the empty sides of vans and minibuses. Such an emptiness extending out, implicitly, forever down the roads in all directions, taking everyone away. There should be something here like memory, like evidence. And pretty soon there was.

And pretty soon it got to where you didn't even have to take it to the customizing shop. You could just buy it off the showroom floor like that. And always pretty much like that—all smeared and airbrushed over the plain original finish with this plain original glimpse into the most perfunctory world—default, uncertain as the landscapes on those science-fiction paperbacks; as thoughtless, arbitrary as the backgrounds in those circus sideshow posters, a suggestion of a world behind the goat-faced boy, for context—ground and sky, a couple of non-specific trees. It got to be a little desperate, maybe. Finally. You would see these hyperillustrated minibuses, every little recess in the sheet metal a cartouche for a separate view of that same formulaic desert, like a conjurer's box turned every which way to show that it's really empty for the miracle—arrival like a magic trick. The gawking, lurching tumbling out at last. The clownlike, freaklike apparition of us here, complete, astonishing. Ta-da. So it became a little crazy. Which is how we do, I guess. Let's crank it up. Let's overdo it. It expanded—or reduced—to a cleanly self-destructive philosophical thrill. The more insistent, more reiterated all that airbrushed bleakness on the outside, the more opulent within— sealed off, contained. It all went velvet plush, shag-carpeted with swivel seats and a TV and a table, even, around which drinks were passed and reassurances and everyone's at home, if only home could be like this. And yet, so strangely, they'd installed, as part of the deal, these bubble windows. Little bug-eyed plastic hemispheres. Domestic space was herniating. Gaping in its splendor at the emptiness. The kids, of course, were drawn to them. They should have sensed the strain, you'd think. The pressure unsustainable. But no. Some kid would have his face in there, hands pressed to the velvet-papered wall, his entire head inside the bubble, all a-goggle, all agape at all that thin translucent distance. Then it burst, like in the movies when the bad guy shoots the window out at thirty-five thousand feet. It all just went—the kid, the drinks, the flocks of playing cards and everything. It all got sucked right out into the yellow afternoon. And that was that. And after a while the murals started to disappear and everything got back to normal.

★

I AM LYING DOWN RIGHT NOW UPSTAIRS AT DUSK FOR A MINUTE, LIS-tening out at the hum of summer insects, and I think I can re-member doing the same thing as a child—my homework done, the TV off, the windows open to the buzzing Texas air and sens-ing such a final emptiness out there. The sound of the whole world with my homework done and the TV off. And my thoughts could not affect it. Such a blankness I could not begin to penetrate. A moment when you find yourself between things, or between ideas of things. The hum of insects like that cloth jerked out from under the table setting—plates and cups and things amazingly left where they are but with the empty space between them captured, as it were, withdrawn, held up for ev-eryone to see. I'm lying here, my homework finished long ago but still this emptiness out there that sounds like insects. With a presence like a cloth pulled out from under everything I can remember—all the particulars left in place, or maybe placeless-ness, unmoved. I should be able to reach them, but there is no space to reach across. It's like a trick. Look—all the objects of your past still there, exactly where they were, but unavailable. Ta-da.

I'm not concerned, nor even competent to be concerned, with Arcosanti's "arcological" goals. Soleri's grandiose ideas. I am concerned with the vast, concrete anticipation he constructed. Not so vast, as so far realized, in actual size—no bigger than an ordinary shopping mall or recreation complex. Although here and there—in the visitors' center and elsewhere if they let you wander about—you'll see the big idea as taken to completion in his drawings and meticulous plastic models, some quite dusty, of the immense, unfolding artichoke-like city of five thousand densely integrated, culturally fluorescent, self-sustaining, and environmentally harmless souls. Which structure would arise from these beginnings and against which these beginnings would seem trivial, and might seem so now if not for the lasagna and the big round concrete windows that take everything in wide-eyed, agape as if surprised to look upon the world; from this initial, vastly open, vastly uncompleted, accidental point of view at the edge of things.

I wonder, when Soleri came here in his later years to visit and to lecture, to review the troops, if he could ever let his mind go quiet at the pause. The sounds of insects. All his homework pretty much done at that point. Sit and take his portion of lasagna. Take a breath and let it go. Consign the theory to the vault. Consider how the air comes through. The little bells ring out their faintly sweet alarm. Oh, are we here yet? Will we be here soon? Have we been here before? Or maybe after? Take it easy. Look at what has happened here. We get a glimpse of our arrival, past and future, all stretched out.

So here's a theory. We are lost. We're neither here nor there. There's you, and there's the you that knows there's you. And in that gap between the two—and we are always in that gap—we're migratory. Back and forth. Like desert pastoralists always crossing and arriving. Somehow never quite arrived. The deep "iambic" Anna Badkhen has observed. The start and stop and start of breath—of aspiration. Never-quiteness, fine-scale longing, as the form our self-awareness takes. It's hard to tell, of course, because it's us. But now and then, I think, we catch an intimation. Something draws the vital emptiness out and shows it to us: Sounds of summer insects. The bewilderment of photographs. That inexplicable void between the earth and sky in children's drawings. What I told my children once, just making it up, about why cicadas make that noise—how they are born containing a vacuum, the gradual admission of air into which propels their mechanism and produces that sound that lasts for days or sometimes weeks until the pressure is equalized and they die.

2

HAVE YOU EVER WATCHED A LITTLE KID ENCOURAGED TO LOOK AT some celestial marvel through a telescope? I'm thinking really young ones, maybe four or five years old. They're not too sure they really want to. It requires their being grasped about the waist and lifted up, presented to it. Most submit to the mechanics, grab the eyepiece like a handlebar and bring their eye up to it and assume that's it, but no, they haven't seen it, haven't looked, don't quite know how. How would they know? There is a pause, a point of stillness, they don't feel quite right about. It's not their business to be still like that—held still yet still awake. To look so narrowly through eyes so wide is risking something almost unendurable. Do you see it, honey? Hold her. Fold her little dress up under, shift your grasp. Her hair is falling in her face. The sounds of grown-ups talking, laughing in the dark. It is too much. But then she's got it. Do you think? Do you see it, honey? Sure she does. The dark, the emptiness. What else? Who knows? But that's it. That's enough. She wriggles free. She's back down playing in the grass. It's like a shot. A vaccination. She can't wait to get back down and run around in the yellow grass, get chased and fall and get the grass all in her hair.

I think it has to be the pause, that pointed, concentrated pause that little kids can't stand when looking through the telescope. Such stillness funneled down like that to hold them in their place. What place? The placelessness, the emptiness they sense inside themselves—that little vacuum they are born with and that, I suspect, is not yet quite sealed off? The fontanelle still slightly open, prone to letting too much in, like an open window—maybe even one of those big, round, rough-cast, un-healed, concrete Arcosanti windows.

Nothing locates you, presumes you to be still, like a tele-scope. The larger ones especially, with those massive, driven, equatorial mounts to compensate for the rotation, the unstill-ness, of the earth. Even the optics seem subordinate to the still-ness. Magnification, useless without it, as deriving from the stillness, almost, rather than the other way around. Look at that photograph of Lowell being held up to his twenty-four-inch refractor (the dimension is the diameter of the lens). It's natural light. So the observatory shutter must be open, and he must be looking at Venus, which he's known to have done in daylight to reduce the planet's glare. He'd mask his huge lens down to a mere three inches, the better to penetrate—peek in between, as it were—the turbulent daytime atmosphere. The whole great instrument squinting. There's such effort. Such a fundamental strain—the whole idea of seeing, longing, brought to bear across such emptiness. And ultimately bringing him such doubt. The spoke-like lines he saw on Venus (possibly shadows of the structures of his retina cast by such a narrow telescopic beam, it's been suggested) he recanted. Later changed his mind again. Regarding Mars, though—the canals, the attribution of intelligence—he'd gone too far to come back down from that, from that apprehension, that deep will to apprehend. So far and still, I want to say, a state of longing as projected through an instrument like that, the smallest psychological inclinations magnified, expanded, mapped, refined beyond the reach of most responsible opinion—though, of course, his maps eventually would be shown to be illusory. A generous mind would find itself out there. Arriving. Longing to arrive. You grasp at things. You look for meaning—that location, that conviction that you think should come with stillness.

3

PHOTOGRAPHS SEEM TO SUGGEST THE POSSIBILITY OF STILLNESS. OF our stillness—as completion. As arrival. That's because what's most conspicuously presented isn't really the subject itself (a painting, after all, does that) so much as the act, the singular fact, of observation. The beholding. The suggestion thus extending to the lens and the photographer whose place you take when looking at a photograph. You think (by now unconsciously, of course, but fundamentally) you're fastened in that place, that observation. You're complicit in that stillness, can't help feeling it's available—and you, your migratory self, resolvable within it. We're all primitives with this. We can't believe it, but it's true because it's random, uncontrived. A photograph—to the extent it's not so tarted up it doesn't look like one—is accidental. Startling. Stumbled upon. Our startlement is buried but it's there.

We do not like it but we keep it—in our wallets or our iPhones. Close to us—the proof of us, our families, pets. We want the proof and bear the startlement. Each time, each ordinary time we take our photos out and show them around, each time I swear we pause upon our desert wandering, our herd of zebu anxious and confused, to think a moment where we are and where proceeding as the lifted dust drifts on ahead like ghosts.

The photograph has no opinion. Notwithstanding the photographer's intention, and, again, to the extent that it's not touched up, hand-colored, messed with as they used to like to do so much with portraits, to suppress, perhaps, that startled sense of randomness, the camera's deep indifference that devalues all to data—there's a chance, after all, that it might be true, as everything else in a photograph seems true. That's how you know that it's a photograph. No inference is required. Whatever we think about the content is external, unimportant to the photograph, the central fact whose simple overwhelming revelation is the thinness of that moment, of our presence in that still and uniform and endless moment, before judgment is imposed. We take core samples with our cameras, random samples—they keep coming back the same. Of course we want to tart them up. Drop phony backgrounds in, apply a little color, deckled edges for that handmade-paper look—and for the artiest chemical photographs these days, you let the edges of the frame creep into the print, enlist, as ornament, the randomness itself to show you mean it, to provide essential value after the fact. Dress up the dead. We can't abide that they are random, we are random, arbitrary, accidental—to the extent more real, more random. To the extent more nearly graspable, possessable: more indistinct, diffuse. That's the bewilderment. The emptiness. The trick. With every photograph you pause with it and reach for it—not consciously, of course, but still you do. And yet there is no point of purchase. Any painted picture's surface is articulate with variable and graspable intention and conviction interacting to extend a thought as simple as *Oh, look*. Whereas the surface of a photograph, beneath what we impute, is unrelieved—conviction uniform, disinterested as glass. Your grasp just slips away. It looks so real, as if such things were real. So you can't help yourself, yet every time you come up empty-handed.

Take, for example, one of those strangely typical nineteenth-century funerary photographs—of the taxidermic style where the departed is dressed up, propped up to join the family group, to return, as it were, from behind the curtain to take a bow. It plays, so clearly and so sadly, to the basic revelation of photography—as if these people know they are reduced to equal value. In order to have their loved one back, they must assemble in a place where living and dead have equal value. Which the photograph—the essential fact of the photograph—provides. The blank-faced child is revived, or else the family group is seen to join her in mortality. In either case the family is reconstituted. Not imagined, wished as in a painting or the mediated contact of the death mask, but demonstrably, indifferently, and truly as whatever enters the photograph is instantly beheld with the same astonished yet disinterested conviction—everything reduced to the fact of itself, one fact as good as another. Point the camera in any direction—it's the same. The tripod kicked, the camera skewed from the family group to take in floral-papered wall, screen door, the bleary, tilted, overexposed beyond—some stubbly cotton field or something—way on out to where the emulsion breaks apart and lets you escape the grief and the cotton field into the understanding that the photographic moment, thin as paper, keeps on going, the essential insubstantial fact with you, your eyes wide open, right on out into the emptiness.

The photographic process is so passive, so inevitable you'd think there must be similar, simple, natural intuitions, revelations all around us all the time. You think of shadows, mirrors, fossils. But these things, one way or another, do not separate from everyday experience—they're not still or they're not passive or not flat. They move with us. We move around them. Or they join the world's activity as projections. They don't fix and represent our observation. Even mirrors do not hold our looking up to us like that. If there were something like a photograph then it would be a photograph. A thing resembling knowing would be knowing.

There seems practically nothing to it. Imagine a cave somewhere, like Plato's in a way, but with a single tiny opening to the outside, through which light, as in a pinhole camera, beams and casts an image onto the opposite wall composed of a mineral substance (I have no idea if such exists in nature) that will fade upon exposure to the light. I'm sure it would require a very long exposure, which would wash out the ephemera—passing nomads, flights of birds—to leave at last, as after a hundred or a hundred thousand years the hole is closed by natural processes, a sort of airbrushed picture in the dark, a photograph of empty landscape. Ground and sky.

Why shouldn't motion pictures amplify the startlement of

photographs? Accumulate it? Overwhelm us with it? Well, at even the most particular, functional level, it refuses to accumulate. Each certainty surrenders to the next, conviction lost to continuity and, finally, to intention, somewhat like that of those rock displays you see sometimes in curio shops where individually striking, primitive chunks of quartz and agate, pyrite, petrified wood, and so forth have been glued onto a board to form a pattern—star or flower or the state of Texas, say—which absolutely kills the bright surprise of each, drawn into service of the ornamental narrative. Motion pictures reassimilate the photograph to ordinary life. The movement seems to be enough to pace experience, let the photographic glance fade into ours the way a lens placed in a liquid of the same refractive index disappears.

Here is a photograph I found among my mother's family pictures years ago, and which I find myself returning to from time to time as it seems to strain so sadly to assimilate, reassimilate, to the world. A little girl in a swing is swinging toward the camera. Just past focus. Blank and round-faced little girl in a plain, pale frock somewhere in Omaha, Nebraska, it is thought. About 1910. I'd guess she's three or four—that anti-telescopic age when the vacuum we are born with still inhabits us with such an active longing. She completely fills the center, squinting straight back at the camera with that blankness children tend to direct toward cameras as if they've been asked a question they can't answer. She's suspended between two fundamental states: at left, these grim dark brick or painted clapboard apartments— very bleak and institutional-looking, from which, one imagines, she's emerged; at right, bleached out in the general overexposure, fading into the blankness of the sky, a field of grass that looks as if it might run out to the edge of the world. She's unendurably suspended. Like the funerary photograph, the content here responds to, sort of brackets, the primitive photographic fact—that unresolvable stillness. Dark, opaque arrival on the one hand; on the other all that clear and grassy migratory emptiness. She's specified yet lost. As lost. She wants to emerge from this, to meet us halfway—look how she swings out toward us, going a little fuzzy, though, as we reach out to take her. We can't help it, even as she starts to blur. What if we nudge her into cinematic motion? Can we bring her into the world that way, yet keep that stark, indifferent specificity? That certainty? Maintain our concentration, our complicity in that moment—our belief in her, essentially? Crank it slowly—just a couple of frames, click, click, completes her movement toward us, blurs her slightly more; we're going to lose her. We are losing concentration. Just that much and we can tell. Now speed it up. She swings away toward focus— Oh my God, a breeze. Across the grass, a little breeze to ruffle her high-cut bangs, her cotton dress—a little too large, inherited probably. Bring it up to standard eighteen frames per second and that's it. The striking, primitive, certain fact of her is washed into the narrative with us. We cannot join her—not, at least, in that still certainty—after all. She blurs away—so we receive her as an analogue of events which, after all, will have to do. She goes from specified-yet-lost to found-yet-generalized. A quantum physics–sounding sort of problem. Our belief in her diffused into belief in a child like that in a moment like that as she swings back and forth like a science demonstration to exhaust some stored potential. It's exhausting. So articulate a photographic moment seems to offer a kind of purchase toward belief. Again and again. Toward resolution out of emptiness. Just look at it—the clarity, the accidental allegory. We can't help but think it should be possible to come to terms with the fact of her on a day like that, in a clean white dress like that in 1910. We can't just leave her. We're compelled to join the fact of that old photograph, to take her from the swing, so gently, carefully— she's us of course, the unlocatable self, let's say the soul; that's part of the allegory—lift her up and fold her white dress under, hold her head against our shoulder as we would, as anyone would, with some lost child in such bleak circumstances. Rock her side to side and feel the breeze and smell the grass and try to comfort her for having to be here so randomly, indifferently. For having the same value as empty landscape.

4

FIVE MONTHS LATER, EARLY AUGUST, AND WE'RE BACK AT ARCOSANTI for a three-day stay in the "Sky Suite." We're not sure what the Sky Suite is, but since the other accommodations seem to constitute that fairly rudimentary sort of barracks down the cliff, we go for this airy-sounding penthouse which, except for a small and, we infer, reluctant portable unit tucked away somewhere in a closet, is unair-conditioned and easy enough to book in the warmer months when it gets well above a hundred. But we're game. And, anyway, that's part of the deal.

This time I'm paying more attention to the approaches—that confusion of construction stuff, cheap plastic outdoor furniture, old vehicles and trailers and containers and equipment rusting away. A stranded camo-painted motor home with a fake twin fifty-caliber machine gun mounted on top. You have to navigate past this to get to parking for the Sky Suite. There's a junkyard; then, between the vaults, this portal to the future. You can't help but want to work it out somehow. Make something of it.

So you pass into the vaults—the Minoan-frescoed vaults where the air, the almost always bright blue air, comes through and people tend to gather; there is evidence of children— through a tunnel on the opposite side, emerging at the top of the amphitheater with its terraced seats descending, half-surrounded by an arc of concrete entrances to apartments or storage spaces, workrooms, who knows, which in turn supports an upper ring, or half ring, of these massive, rough-cast, forked, concrete projections that, without (for so many years, you think, without) the great domed canopy or roof they must be reaching for, have let the sky fall in and reabsorbed that thrust of purpose into another, automatically it seems, becoming flat, schematic, gaping heads of animals. Quite naturally, like wolves or Quetzal-coatls. Let things go and you get animals. You know. The sky falls in and you get animals.

The Sky Suite is above the ring of animals at the south end of a higher tier of structures. Unspectacular but bright and many-windowed, giving views across the valley to the south and east and, strangely—through a glazed port in the kitchen— into quarters just below: a glimpse of someone's back steps down there. Where they leave their shoes and come and go out onto their little terrace right outside your bedroom window in the mornings, so you need to close your curtain on arising if you care. Things interpenetrate in odd, surprising ways. Inten-tions seem to shift and vanish at this level far below the higher orders of Soleri's great recivilizing vision. From which, now, it seems this place has been released to drift, upon residual impulse into the future. I suspect that most living here don't care too much. They do not think about it that way. That the future, in and of itself, might finally be the point. They simply go about their business. Put their shoes on by the steps and have their lives here. Raise their children, in some cases. Which you don't see very often. For some reason. Mostly evidence, as I say— tricycles, toys around the edges of the vaults which make an easy, open play space I should think when no one's looking. When they're not expecting tours. The interpenetrating processes of things—part of the general ambiguity you get here in the future, I suppose. What you sense just walking around is that at any point it's all about to change its mind. Small changes here and there recorded in the concrete seem to reveal a certain built-in vacillation at a fundamental level—points of pause, reflection, "What in the world are we doing?"—as it all gets sort of balanced on the moment. Here and there it might have gone the other way. Is this the blurry edge you get as things are nudged into the future? Or just how it goes as notions change and people change their minds and fall away. The kids get older and you're not sure what to do. What in the world to make of this?

I like the rough, round-fenestrated concrete panels everywhere. Most very large. It is exotic in this context, futuristic. And it's structurally efficient. And you find you're looking through it all the time. And mostly south across the valley—or the canyon, what to call it? That dry wash down there that's made a gulf to gaze across. To sort of squint as through a lens, a telescope, and think, *Well, there's the future maybe, somehow.* Actual future, as it were. Where the answering bells of cattle may be heard returning home someday and we shall all be gathered to a place of perfect, strangely perfect, stillness and arrival. By and by.

At home in a little downstairs room devoted, more or less, to scientific odds and ends I have a strange device my friend Chuck Watson and I built years ago to detect heretofore undiscovered signals from Mars. It's called The Mars Receiver and, although of course it doesn't work, it makes a pretty good show which, since I was a child, seems to have been enough for me. Toward what, remains the question. It attempts to recapitulate, with no more rationality and yet with real mechanical and electrical components linked in immediately rational ways, my childhood efforts, made of cardboard and repurposed parts of anything lying around, to duplicate the device employed by Peter Graves in *Red Planet Mars*—an exceedingly goofy science-fiction movie from 1952 whose religious message I found tedious but whose instrumentation, captivating. What sort of nonsense is this? I'm not sure I know. Nor even whether there's a sort to which it belongs. But at that time, that winter I think, my wife having finally left for good, and Chuck, once more between those quite impressive engineering jobs that somehow never lasted, having come to stay in my son's old room for a while; and I, having not too long before having had occasion to visit the sixteenth-century mathematician and astronomer John Dee's famous crystal ball in the British Museum, that same curiously small dim sphere of smoky quartz whereby, in that era's heady confusion of religion, magic, and science, he had sought, with the questionable aid of the occultist Edward Kelley (whose birthday, I might add, Chuck shares) to consult with angels; and the weather all gone cold and wet, opaque for weeks it seemed to me, it seemed to me a good idea to revisit that old nonsense, that old thing, to see if one might manage to clarify or penetrate the silliness, the hopelessness, enlist it, with Chuck's help, his special knowledge, to communicate with Mars.

Well, first of all it had to look good. Through my wintry, sad opacity of mind it had to glow. Give forth that clear, intuitive, radiant sense of functional intercession. Get the faceplate—heavy aluminum; no more cardboard—going first. Establish that. The circular screen, the lights and toggle switches. Then attend to theory or whatever passes for it. One can always plead conceptual art, of course. Concept or no. But that's not it. Chuck understood. Start with a beautiful thing, then bring the angels to it.

Back before Chuck got depressed and went nomadic, he worked quite a number of years in electro-optics for an outfit called E-Systems outside Dallas. He recalled a particular project to create a means to parse and render instantly intelligible vast sectors of entangled air traffic transponder information that presented such a problem for controllers in identifying aircraft in a very crowded sky. What this involved—so oddly it seemed to me—was passing a laser beam through a slab of lab-grown quartz as it was acted upon, vibrated, by a transducer (the active component in a speaker) responding to audio output generated by a system of antennas, filters, and amplifiers tuned to the tangle of signals. Thus was set up in the quartz immensely complex patterns of sound waves, which meant rapidly, microscopically, varying densities and therefore optical qualities, which caused the laser beam to deflect in a sort of pantographic way to expand and articulate all that confusion into instant legibility—as passed, of course, from sensor to computer. Holy crap, I think I said— the daylight fading, drizzle starting to turn to sleet, as I remembered a real quartz crystal ball I'd put away somewhere—can we do that? Can we produce some sort of pattern on a cathode-ray tube screen (which you could still get, as a small TV, back then) that might, with not unreasonable hope, hooked up to some receptive-looking, outward-gazing-across-the-emptiness antenna sort of thing, be felt to display effects of subtle emanations from beyond? Perhaps not angels, nor the voice of God that Peter Graves tuned in to. Something, though. The not quite zero probability.

At one point with the faceplate shaping up—we'd got the lights (blue, red, and green) and the toggle switches mounted under the big round screen (an eight-inch hole rough-sawn and filed out of the heavy eighteen-by-twenty-inch aluminum plate)—so it looked like a giant oscilloscope, and the TV tube still dangling all its original TV parts, we plugged it in to see how the screen, now round and fitted into a context of such scientific potency, might look turned on. I think it was some sitcom—nothing to it. People sitting on a couch. But it was startling. Oh my God. The first TV. The first round, arbitrary glimpse into such a thing. The cool, unsympathetic gaze. We left it on. Went out for barbecue or something. Peeked back in from time to time to verify our inexplicable astonishment. The beauty and the terror of it. Images beheld—it didn't matter what—in such constraining purity, it all went scientific like a sample, like a specimen of something never seen before, of people sitting, mugging on a couch, of car commercials. One is distanced, properly distanced, by the instrument. You can't pretend it's furniture. Or theater. You take it in wide-eyed like that.

A mystery. I remember as a kid I'd sometimes visit my friend Greg Cotter's grandmother Mary, who lived down the street. She and her husband had come from Buffalo, New York, and I suppose I must have actually paid attention to her stories, for I have, as if a memory of some previous life, what feels like such a dense, extended sense of Buffalo despite having never been there. Dark and snowy, empty parks, old white frame houses. Mostly cold. And I remember in the corner of her living room an ancient TV set—so dark and cold I assumed it had to have come from Buffalo. A tiny dark green screen almost an afterthought, conceding to the human need to witness marvels only with reluctance rendered visible within that great cathedral-like enclosure. It was never on. I doubt it even worked. And I could not imagine watching it with anything but doubt. No one had ever felt inclined to get all comfy in front of that with a bowl of popcorn, I was sure. Yet it suggested something wonderful and strange. That what I loved and took for granted, took to be a natural window, once emerged in chill obscurity, uncertainty, to penetrate the dead-gray sky of Buffalo, New York, with what would likely have been almost unintelligible to me. I'm pretty sure I never asked her if it worked. I might have feared to see what *Beat the Clock* or *I Love Lucy* looked like small, obscure, and green as radium. The distance of it might have been unbearable. What are we really gazing at across the gulf like that?

So here I'm primed. I get a framing shop to cut a round black mat a little smaller than the hole in the aluminum to finish out the look and make a gasket to protect the tube. Chuck finds a pair of rheostats with nice big knobs—for audio and laser— scores a gorgeous vintage meter at a swap meet. I'm in charge of the crystal ball. I know, I know, it gets pathetic. I can't tell if I miss my wife. The girls are here. John's off to college. That's my son, whose room we're using as a lab. There is no theory. There is longing and regret and self-indulgence. Which may not be quite enough.

How strange, after all this time, to retain that sense of Buffalo, New York, as representing cold and distant and uncertain. At the edge of my dreams sometimes. The empty parks. What's that about? It feels like Mars. That's where we go to try to find ourselves, I guess. We go to Buffalo or Mars.

This whole thing takes a while. The season changes, brightens. Life intrudes. The moment dissipates. The crystal-laser setup doesn't work. The crystal ball—the size of a baseball—is too massive or too flawed. Chuck thinks too massive—flaws in the crystal should only help make it interesting. And they do as far as it goes. The laser shining through makes a lovely, shifting kaleidoscopic pattern as delivered by a tiny TV camera to the screen as the ball—on its worm-geared mount inside—is turned this way or that by means of a very nifty indexed knob to make it tunable, to index certain "sweet spots" we imagined might reveal themselves. But nothing reveals itself—and here I'm only talking practically, internally, of course. Reception of signals from beyond—the ultimate working of the thing—is far from our thoughts these days and falls under very different rules of evidence.

A little crystal ball I get from a rock shop works no better. You can crank the audio all the way up on that big black 1950s Collins radio receiver we've hooked up. You can hear the crystal actually buzzing. But that's it. There's no deflection of the laser. Or the meter, for that matter. Hope and longing flicker and dim. I have Tim Coursey make a cabinet for it anyway. Industrial gray. It's beautiful. No angels though. The silliness, the hopelessness, at best refined a little. It's a conversation piece: You see, we thought we'd try to communicate with Mars—not actually Mars, of course, but Mars as a sort of metaphor for something. (At this point you flip the toggle switches—one, two, three as, one, two, three the little lights come on and there's a crackling from the screen, which is the metaphor uncrumpling like a piece of cellophane.) Don't even bother turning on the massive Collins 388, it's not really worth the time it takes to warm it up. Nor to tune past all those religious stations that have pretty much taken over the shortwave bands. Just turn that little indexed knob to show how the focus of the laser, overexposed to white at the center of the screen, flares out bright red to the edge in shifting rays and dusty-looking clouds as the crystal turns, sometimes resolving into arrays of brilliant spots suggesting structural, even molecular, alignments in the quartz. But it's just you. You're doing it all. You turn the knob. It doesn't count, you explain. It's pretty, but that's all. No information leaks across. No sensitivities set up as natural, visible fluctuations in the system to encourage the possibility, non-zero probability, of darker and more distant understandings lurking somewhere in the static, in the dust, across the wash, the bleak Sahel, the empty parks, whatever that means, up there in Buffalo, New York, extending on and on, it felt like in those dreams, right into space as if we might just walk on out there in our sleep, from under the dark and snowy trees right into space.

5

WHAT DO WE DO WITH THAT AMBIVALENCE, THAT NEITHER-HERE-NOR-
thereness that both haunts us and enables us to be ourselves, to
know ourselves—to situate ourselves, as it seems, so strangely in
the fact of our dispersion? Like that little girl in the photograph,
our longing to believe in her, imagine her to be real, picked up
and held, we grasp ourselves to find we're generalized, extended,
unresolved. So what we do, I think, is look for us. Continuously.
Seek evidence for us. Seek to converge, as it were—arrive. Some
old, preconscious hunting instinct operating to direct us round
and round in widening circles, Elmer Fudd–like on the trail of
our own footprints. And the wider the circles, the fainter the
spoor, the more exhilarating (in those moments when we notice) the whole process that emerges in the gap—that splitting,
duplicating principle in us that finds duplicity in everything,

which is to say finds meaning. Once we mean ourselves, the rest must follow: language, God, and so forth. Wider and wider, round and round. And yet why should the attenuation—which you'd think would disperse our hopes—seem to expand them? Why, when we find ourselves addressing some great vista all of a sudden—driving home from Colorado, say, in the Volvo station wagon with the family and the baggage and the fast-food mess and Kim Carnes's "Bette Davis Eyes" condensing out of the high, thin air so weirdly and portentously and sadly over the radio exactly as you crest the final snowy ridge and find yourself presented to this vast, imponderable distance, as your gaze drifts into Kansas and your sense of where you are just falls away and swoops on out to the very edge of things, like all your breath drawn out, your heart drawn out—why, when that happens, is it thrilling?

The Fulani nomads Anna Badkhen traveled with spend their whole lives on their own trail. Dispersing themselves in every sense. "As if they journeyed not simply across distance but across eras and dragged with them through the land grooved with prehistoric cow paths all the cattle and all the herders who had laid tracks here before." Whatever isn't ground or sky acquires a preciousness. Grass, twigs, manure. And plastic. These days, plastic—colorful fabrics, flip-flops, bags and buckets. Bright though fading, limited half-life plastic introduced into this clear and ancient process like an isotope, like a radioactive tracer into the bloodstream to reveal in greater detail the circulation. To fluoresce the trail within the blur of footprints, plot the progress of desire so thin, it seems, so close to the earth, it tends to vanish. These "spent teabags, broken flipflops, slivers of cracked plastic" don't dissolve back into the emptiness the way our small affections and attachments ought to do. They leave a trace like the phosphor trail of an oscilloscope. Like longing. Like those artificial flowers you wish people wouldn't leave out there in the cemetery—much too sad and eloquent, too slow to fade to white; and even then, and even crumbled into powder, there's a residue, a half-life of regret you can't get rid of, can't imagine in a million years reprocessed into something fundamental, prior to meaning, prior to loss. The Fulani spread themselves too thin to ever be quite here or there. And in the thinnest rainy season in a while, in Anna's narrative *Walking with Abel,* they're so dusty, so like dust they seem about to blow away, just sitting there. Dispersed in place. Old Oumarou sits in despair on a sheet of black plastic near the end, turned away from the river where he'd lost a cow that day—three animals lost already this season. He seems turned away from everything at this point, from the land as well where—how many?—wives and children had been buried along the way. Why would he sit on a sheet of black plastic like a body bag laid out for him? Although dispersed in principle, unbaggable, his dusty fears and sorrows seem to collect upon it. What in the world is that about? That plastic out in the desert, in the cemetery? How it seems so gaudily to bond to our affections, to stand for something that refuses to resolve. The trail of something not quite natural, undegradable, unresolvable in us. We wish old Oumarou would go sit somewhere else.

★

I LOVED TO HANG OUT IN THE ALLEYS AS A KID. OF COURSE, A KID would. Kids love undiscovered places. And the alleys of the simplest 1950s postwar neighborhoods were deeply undiscovered. More obscure than those of Istanbul or Victorian London's terrifying secret penetrations, I feel sure, because so open, so laid out, exactly because so clearly prescribed as if on some mysterious instruction from the earth. The war is over, chaos banished, here is how we all shall live. And, for the moment, all the same. Upon this newly mapped-out world. The whole low-rooflined, gridded, nearly treeless world (that little elm or whatever it was in our first front yard here in Dallas, I was told my father yanked, himself, from the muddy banks of the Trinity), but the whole flat world was about as new as we. We kids. At four or five, in those days, we could wander about on our own pretty much, as if in our own mind. And how the narrow, unpaved alleys seemed to run right through our sense of things, straight through our little open skulls, the fontanelles that, I suspect, don't ever really close. The holes in our heads we never lose.

I have before me on my desk in a perfectly chosen, overly fancy wooden frame a little five-by-seven-inch tempera or acrylic-painted dioramic model of a simple suburban neighborhood that Nancy bought for a dollar a couple of years ago at a Corsicana flea market. Here is evidence of us, somehow, of a special kind I think. Twelve tiny plastic Monopoly houses—I suppose Monopoly houses, identical markers, square with low-pitched roofs and narrow eaves and little round sprues on top to stand for chimneys—six on either side of a painted street with painted bright green yards and dark green trees and red-brown smudges for garages, with the streaky, muddy-looking light gray alleys running behind. It's all that dead-flat chalky paint with no relief except for the houses and the topographic warping of the watercolor paper. One assumes some sort of school project. But who knows? It appears complete as is. The painting stops at the edge. It's done. No more to say. No label, signature, or date. Except for the swimming pools—four gloppy, light blue, free-form, one rectangular, with scribbled ballpoint diving boards—it might be my old neighborhood. The pools, though, probably make it 1970s or later. Still, it serves. The dry, flat surface sucks you in and takes you right back to that level. That beginning of the world.

Someone has hovered over this. Has thought about it. As coarse and smudgy as it is—you sense the brush held in the fist—there is a care. A tongue-protruding concentration on particulars. Not just the tiny swimming pools but every smudgy tree—straight thalo green straight out of the tube, brush pressed straight down onto the paper—seems intended to transfer essential fact from an actual noon-lit summer day seen from above. From some unknowable, blurry, possibly interplanetary distance with the aid of some great telescope. Look here. There must be people here. We believe these lines are alleys or streets—those small bright features, pools of liquid water.

Not every yard will have a tree—though usually a bush or two. A touch of violet here and there right up against the house to stand for flowers. And a couple of odd details where the perfunctory hand appears to have gotten caught in the finer moment, something known, remembered: Someone's got a boat out back. By the alley—scribbled ballpoint like the diving boards, or no; adjusting focus, that's not ballpoint, that's the sharp end of the handle of the brush dipped in gray paint to scratch these fainter observations in, the diving boards, the fences, and this boat behind the pool, next to a white-glopped concrete slab, next to the alley. There's a gray-scratched gate left open to the alley. For the boat to slip out that way, I suppose. No one to notice, down the alley to the lake.

I've got it lying flat right here next to the legal pad I write on, under my desk light. I can change the time of day by moving the desk light, which is on a flexible arm. I'll bend it slowly down to the left, the west—it feels to me like west—and watch the shadows of the tiny houses angle across the drives, across the fences into the tiny yards next door, and feel the tiniest emotion in myself. A miniature of that regret you feel at evening—used to feel, it seemed, so clearly in such simple circumstances, all the shadows angling, lengthening the same across all yards, into all windows, darkening rooms. You catch your breath a tiny bit at the detail. The weird, exhilarating accuracy. How can a thing like that, the fully felt detail like that, be concentrated on this little printed circuit? This cuneiform-like tablet? There is meaning. There is evidence and loss at every scale. At every moment. I can make it feel like sunset spilling across my legal pad. I can't believe I'm actually doing this—I hover, bring my face down close, the desk light slowly down into the west with a silly creaking sound. I can't believe how truly sad this is.

The other day I took a drive back to that neighborhood where we first lived in Dallas. It's still pretty much the same except our little white frame Monopoly house on the corner is gone, replaced by one much larger, with a cedar fence extending around the back, which sort of messes up the feeling of things there right by the alley. That's the view I wanted—back behind the garage and down the alley. Which remains unpaved, at least. Gray, chalky, crumbly Dallas dirt—that hasn't changed. Which seems amazing. That that chalky, vague default that runs straight through me hasn't changed. How strange, you'd think, to keep so blurry and uncertain, almost empty, an idea—or not idea; one didn't make ideas till later—but so vague a thought, a feeling, all these years. And yet there was a sharpness to it. Which I did encounter once. Clear and precise as it could be. As things can be when you are only five or so. I'm in the alley poking around. As you're allowed. You're into everything. You understand already everything back here is lost. It's up for grabs. It's probably summer, probably early afternoon. You never know what you might find. Or having found it, what it means. But this is what you do at five years old. You look for stuff in undiscovered places, in the emptiness, beneath a bright blue sky, at the beginning of the world. You reach way down into that garbage can for something—surely something. And you pluck it out and find you have been wounded by it. Reaching in like that without a thought. Without a clear idea. A piece of deep blue—cobalt blue, Noxzema blue it seems now—broken glass. I think it probably had that deep medicinal smell. My God. I think now of the terror of the war and all the young men like my father coming home to this sweet diagram. And all that terror never really banished, just subsided. Worked back in. Implicit right here in the bright blue afternoon. It's like I'm wounded just for being here. You don't know how to take pain in exactly, so it's as if it belongs to the glass, that color like the concentrated color of the sky. The risk you take when you just go for things. At least in Lorca's famous poem the emptiness is ringed—there is a boundary. "*A las cinco de la tarde,*" "when the bull ring was covered with iodine at five in the afternoon." "Oh, white wall of Spain! Oh, black bull of sorrow!" Oh, at least that seems contained. But here I'm bleeding in the alley, which is endless, from a little wound so clear, precise, implicit, I can feel it still. It never goes away.

6

THIS MAY BE WHERE I NEED TO LAY THINGS OUT REGARDING HOW DIF-
fuse I am. Have always been. Like poor old Oumarou but much
less honorably somehow. Much less naturally. Less inevitably.
Diffuse as in preliminary, unconsolidated. Superficial. Very scattered in my interests—and those interests, for the most part, in
the surfaces of things. The superficial look and feel of things
and, if pretending any depth at all, what look and feel convey
toward deeper understandings. How depth shines upon the surface. And it does. It's the idea of depth that shimmers like an oil
slick to the surfaces of things and sort of stops me. Dazzles. Eyes
go goofy spirals. Mr. Toad–like. As if all were in appearances.
And all, therefore, more concentrated, meaningful, compressed
into the flatness of that shine. God's grandeur rendered as the
"shining from shook foil" in Hopkins's phrase, which I have fi-

nally learned to love. The cheapest, thinnest, flashiest is, of course, most potent, most direct.

I can remember trying to learn Morse code in order to deserve to have a shortwave radio set. To get to have it. Have the look of it, the presence of that potency—the dials and lights and switches (I know, I know, nothing changes), all that gaudy intercession like some foiled and tinseled image of the Virgin. I remember actually studying it like Hebrew. It was hopeless. Twelve years old, I think, and taken after dark to a place—some rude and temporary sort of structure near a radio station somewhere—to be tested with the others. Shadowy others, mostly young. Did we wear earphones? I'm not sure. In any case, it was this beeping in my ear like someone rapping on a pipe. Intrinsic urgency that seemed to overwhelm interpretation. As I imagine Hebrew might in certain exegetical circumstances. Dahs and dits of deepest, most elusive practical meanings I'd no gift for. I just couldn't get it down. A broken phrase or two, perhaps. An S.O.S. Dear God I'm sinking. This is depth and I've no use for it. Just get me to the surface. Take me home.

About this time I joined the Boy Scouts. Here again, responsibility convened in a perfunctory sort of barracks, in this case behind a church. The Bat Patrol, which sounded pretty cool, I guess. I liked the patch. One got outfitted at a little glass-topped counter in a corner of a local clothing store—all ranks and orders, decorations, celebrations of achievement on display. One's head inclined above the glass. I don't believe we had a list, a proper order form or anything. My mom and I. My dad was very busy. And I doubt whoever served us had authority or knowledge in these matters—someone filling in, I'm sure. With the result that, on the evening of our induction, I arrive, dropped off a little late, and make my way past the assembled to my seat as a sort of field marshal, Lord High Webelos or something quite spectacular as signified (especially egregiously, I'd later be informed) by the gorgeous golden loop of braid upon my shoulder and God knows what else. Supreme Allied Commander. I had synthesized some rank undreamt of. Had there been a saber, I'd have worn it. I was rank. All rank. Epitome of rank. A shimmering mockery of rank. Appropriation of the symbols. Marlon Brando with that stolen trophy strapped to the front of his motorcycle. Wild Alaric gleaming in insignia of slaughtered legions. All distinctions, deeper understandings, garbled, lost in primal dazzle. Past deserving. Past transcription and translation. What's so funny is they let me sit there like that for the program. Till I think I must have thought it's going to be okay. This Boy Scout stuff. It might turn out all right. But then, of course, at last, I'm taken aside and sternly, gently stripped, reduced and sent into the night.

I did stay with it for a little while. I learned to tie some knots, made Second Class, whose fragile curl of ribbon seemed a less impressive badge than even the Tenderfoot's, and finally just stopped going. And so cursed myself forever with that faint and fluttery banner borne before me all my life. A sort of wind spreads out away from me. My little pennant flaps without direction—second class, for second take, for that self-duplicating startlement, that mirroring involved in all the shiny, gaudy, spiral-eye-inducing apprehensions of the world, the cheap shook foil of our amazement. I collect things now, and put them in glass cases so they cannot blow away. Antique ray guns. Giant beetles. Asian pots and meteorites and rocket engines. Still, it seems, one's head inclines above the glass.

★

WHAT IN THE WORLD WAS JOHN DEE DOING? THAT REMARKABLE sixteenth-century proto-scientific mind. The mathematician and advisor to the queen. What was he doing, gazing into that little smoky crystal ball—or not even gazing himself but having Edward Kelley do it for him? In order to what? Consult with angels? Really? What must it have been like then, the force of barely discovered rationality brought to engage the whole accumulated dark irrational world as if with a better kind of magic. How bewildering, terrifying and, perhaps, exhilarating. Everything—the vast uncritical mass of human fear and longing—still, for the moment, served as plausible and compressible into the forms, at least, of reason. I've a photograph tipped into Deborah Harkness's *John Dee's Conversations with Angels* (Cambridge, 1999) of his "shewstone" on its little plastic rock-shop stand in the British Museum. There's a shadow, a reflection, of me in it. Or an angel—hard to say. It's very dim. I was surprised that they don't mind photographs so long as you don't flash. But there's this dark, hunch-shouldered figure I suppose is me dead center with reflections of the other magical contents of the case—obsidian mirror (not John Dee's, according to Harkness), magically figured beeswax seals, gold disk with visionary inscription, and the room itself I had to be directed to, all wrapping round in spherical distortion. The whole world, of course in principle, wrapping round. Were there no walls and were it night and it were clear, you would see stars, the shape of space distorting, wrapping round within, upon, the sphere. (The polished fingernails of virgins, Harkness notes, might serve as well.) The simplest thing. The simple shiny intercession of it. You just let your thoughts go. Let the sky fall in, as it were, and what do you get? Well, sometimes animals, I guess; but sometimes angels. If it's beautiful and shiny, you get angels. That dark smudge could be an angel.

I suspect that, given a certain concentrating state of mind, you sense a vacuum is created. With the world compressed like that, into that space, you sense the emptiness it has to have left behind. The potent emptiness around you, not unlike the potent emptiness within, and into which the ordinarily inadmissible is drawn. And then referred—as the outer emptiness refers to the inner—into the crystal ball. Don't you imagine? I can imagine that might be the way it operates. Is it you or an angel there? That strange slump-shouldered little smudge. Late in December at that latitude the sun begins to set midafternoon. My wife—who very soon will leave me for the last time, and I think I probably know it—and my daughters are still jet-lagged and sleeping in our flat, or possibly waking into the vacuum. Though my son, who's made some friends, is out and about. And I am left to track down John Dee's crystal ball in which, in my present state of mind, in the gathering dark, I find, as in Wallace Stevens's anecdotal jar, the "slovenly wilderness" of the world is darkly ordered. I am dazzled, even so. My head inclines, my camera up against the glass. "The angel Anael," says Harkness, "instructed Dee to communicate with the angels on 'the brightest day, when the Sonne shyneth. . . . In the Sonne set the stone.'" I sense, perhaps especially in this darkly ordered place, sun going down, no flash allowed, the glare awaiting in that murky little sphere. So, simply place it in the sun and that angelic smudge will blaze forth like a—what? An afterimage? At the verge of blindness, maybe. Visual circuits overloading. One's own physical limitations in support of the effect—the retinal structure, personal longing, as with Lowell from that little chair. As if you have to risk the possibility that it might be only you and not the other. That celestial thing out there.

7

FROM DALLAS I AM OFF TO ARIZONA AGAIN. THIS TIME I'VE MADE THE proper arrangements at Lowell Observatory for a tour of the dome and the twenty-four-inch refractor, both undergoing restoration and removed from view as we discovered earlier. Which was before I'd begun to write whatever this is—but now I have and find it's useful to announce that I'm doing a book. I'll spend a couple of days with Nancy at her daughter's house in Tempe, where she's been for several weeks to help with Theodore, first grandchild, nine months old. Then we'll take off on an expedition to a number of sites out there that I suspect will figure into the book, although not all in ways I've figured out.

Our stay in Tempe seems to work as a sort of calibrating pause. This clear and simple, necessary little neighborhood— these 1950s houses, like Monopoly houses, just enough to hold the thought. What thought? There is a thought. A sort of diagram, in fact. (Perhaps not unlike that which Lowell imposed upon the planet Mars—the thinnest, clearest subconscious overlay.) These houses, yards, and alleys seem to me exactly adequate to us—our lives, our sensing of our lives. The face of the earth, the blank expanse articulated, schematized. We walk the dogs. We put the kid down for his nap. We read and write and toss the Frisbee for the Frisbee-crazed Australian cattle dog mutt. We sit on the porch and watch the weather. In the afternoon young Theodore and I, he in his wheeled containment, take a little trip around the backyard, stopping here and there—by the orange tree, in the patch of dirt by the alley near the poison oleander. I will place him on the ground and squat beside him. Oh my goodness, I remember. These primordial fascinations. Oh my God. The dirt, the alley, and the danger held implicit in the poison oleander.

Once again, halfway to Flagstaff we stop off at Arcosanti. Nancy wants to buy a little bell for Theodore. I simply want to have another look at the rough-cast concrete—pocked and stone-included ground sides of the panels facing out into the glare of the afternoon. It's like an abrasion that needs bandaging. The pure idea so sensitive, so vulnerable exposed like that—that raw, unfinished interface with ground exposed to air. The pure idea impressed on ground, derived from ground, yanked free like ochre-stenciled Magdalenian handprints on the rock. As soon as the future is imagined, it's imagined somehow ancient. There's this strain involved. Is that what I found so exhilarating, so bewildering, exciting, and expanding or dispersing in that science-fiction paperback cover art so long ago? A strain to hold yourself together in the moment of extension? Understand how thoughts of future and of past may propagate at similar frequencies? That once released the here and now expands in all directions like a gas.

Three in the afternoon just blazes off the futuristic wounded-looking concrete of the visitors' center complex. Those round-fenestrated cubes. The ancient earthy, heavy notion of geometry—the raw, mundane idea of pure idea—admitted to in those abstractions. Here's the future caught in ordinary light. Eroding blue-skied, cirrus-clouded afternoon that blasts away at pure idea. An older couple strolls about. They're in no hurry, pausing here and there like cemetery visitors. Late seventies, early eighties, I would guess—that age at which one's fading, corrugating self begins to find some reassurance, hope of clarity in renewables, the redbud tree next to them in my photograph, the freshness of their clothes. As we ascend toward pure idea, they make me think, we all get blasted, contradicted, if we're lucky toward some residue of clarity.

We're about an hour late to the observatory. All is well, however. We've a kind and patient guide in young Josh Bangle from Communication and Marketing. He makes time for us. He has the keys to everything. It might require some fumbling in the gloom but all eventually will open into the preparatory, unassembled state of things that must come close to how it was at the refractor's installation. I imagine. Such an earthy-feeling structure (here again), the dome—or not an actual hemispherical dome but, rather, this blunted cone, this great inverted bucket, very barnlike, very expedient and pragmatic. What's the most straightforward, least elaborate way to get the biggest, clearest space to put a lot of something basic in—a pure idea, a telescope, a season's hay stacked up, swung in straight through the observation slit, the lacy wooden bracing all around it all exposed and all to purpose. I think maybe I seek agricultural origins in everything. Especially the scientific gesture—something in the clear exposures of the farmer and the scientist feels very much the same. The same clear, grounded, slightly fearful elevation of the gaze.

For a while in my early teens I belonged to a local astronomy club (no qualifying rigors, at the junior level anyway) that maintained a small observatory south of town on a little hill in rural Ellis County where the night skies were, in those days, fairly dark. The simple twenty-one-foot cylindrical base was cinder block, the "dome" a wood-frame composition-covered cone with an undramatic flat, hinged door like a storm-shelter entrance over the narrow observation slit. I found this homely practicality regretful, though the big twelve-inch reflector it contained was pretty impressive on its massive German equatorial mount with its Jules Vernian complications and requiring that you climb a rickety ladder to look through it. There was something wonderfully laborious and even a little risky about it—hauling in the heavens as mechanically as stacking feed for winter. I am able to recall no actual view—no clear transporting glimpse—through the eyepiece as young amateurs might generally be expected to experience. Save once—and this so strained and faint it hardly seems to count—when David Bradbury, somewhat older than the rest of us and vastly more invested and devoted, brought his beautiful, home-built, ten-inch, fully motorized Newtonian to the site and, with the aid of special charts and arcane knowledge, managed to bring the dim, and still to us abstract and almost mythical, planet Pluto into the field. You had, at least I had, to use "averted vision"—that technique whereby you catch the apparition in the corner of your eye. Pretend to look away. Not care. Allow your thoughts to drift, the presence of the others crowding, waiting, to recede, "and feel the breeze and smell the grass" and there it is. The faintest speck against the dark wherein a world is represented.

Anyway, it was no more than a couple of years before my interest faded and I drifted off myself, and civilization, with its streetlights and its vandalism, drifted into rural Ellis County, with the result that the big reflector was removed in the early seventies and the site itself abandoned a few years later. It was not until the summer of 2000 that I thought to return to see if I could even find the hill, what might be left. I had been doing these oddly studious, oddly meaningless pencil drawings of Mars from photographs I'd taken through my own twelve-inch reflector during the close approach (the opposition) of 1988. No practical reason for them—unlike when you do it at the eyepiece, where it's possible (or once was, in predigital times) to catch those fleeting features that the camera can't record. No information to be gained in this case. I was simply grinding out impressions of impressions—as a kind of reintention, I suppose (they were my photographs at least), and trying not to make improvements, but to draw the blur as if it *were* essential information. I was probably still fiddling with The Mars Receiver too. And dealing with a certain blurring of my own life at that point. When it occurred to me to wonder if, after all these years, there might be something out there to identify. And, sure

enough, there was. I love concentric tales. The drawing of the
drawing or the drawing of the photograph. The stories drawn
within each other—once you let the artifice become the ground,
the whole idea of ground becomes the story, the excuse, and
you can just keep on like that. Each tale, impression, becoming,
as in *The Thousand and One Nights,* a ground, a desert even insofar as it permits that emptiness, that deep discontinuity between
the layers. Exactly as the self gives up to find itself again, the
meaning seems to arise in the gap, the glance away. A case, I
hope, for being "scattered." In a chapter wonderfully titled "The
Discovery of Meaning" in his study of medieval French and
English narrative form, *The Rise of Romance,* the Arthurian
scholar Eugène Vinaver describes how, in the mid-twelfth
century, narrative began to question itself toward that self-
understanding that would come to be known as literature. At
the same time music began, in the art of polyphony, to interro-
gate itself, and "the marriage of [secular narrative] matter and
meaning" occurred. A sort of literary talking to oneself. Interior
monologue erupts in a kind of mitosis, story splits along reflec-
tive planes to discover, for the first time since antiquity, a sense
of itself within itself, the theme, the deeper meaning in the gap.
It opens up, you feel the breeze, and there it is.

So off I go to Ellis County and I find it. Not right off. It
takes a while. I just head out. I leave my strange, redundant
drawings and proceed without attempting to research it, in the
middle of the August afternoon to see if I can rediscover that old
route before the highways, sort of feel my way out to it (Might
that service station be the one—or once have been the one—all
by itself out here that marked where one should turn?) but find

myself uncertain finally thinking maybe this is it, the trees, the dipping of the road, all else erased, or maybe not (so hard to tell; the light is wrong; we never came out here in the blazing afternoon), so back and forth down other narrow asphalt roads that dip through subtle possibilities confused by tasteful urban residential fillings-in till there it is. Like Mayan ruins. Like Palenque—strangely futuristic ruins unencroached upon somehow except by grass and vine and hackberry tree and notions of the Waste Land in Arthurian romance. Up there on the hill—not much of a hill; a little rise—to crumble away in all that chatter of insects like some whispery malediction. All that insect noise fills all the space between the way it is and how it was or might have been or shall have been. Or something. Standing in the weeds you lose your tenses. Such a rush and pulse of insect noise you get here in the summer like there's something wrong, almost. It gets so loud, could get so loud, your kids would ask, What is that? Well, you say, that is the sound of the present moment leaking away—the tiny vacuum at the center of each insect, each cicada, equalizing. All those tiny present moments fading out. Which all adds up. All that remains up here is cinder block with its rusted angle-iron cap and the massive concrete pier in the middle. Now completely overgrown inside and out. Whole trees established.

Nine years later on a silent winter morning I return and it's cleaned up. The grass is cut, the brush cleared out. A sign declares that it has become a ranch for "Registered Longhorn Cattle," and the old observatory is still there—restored, in fact. A shingled (non-rotating) conical roof with a weather vane on top. I will discover, on the *Blog for Ellis County Texas History,* that it's used for storing feed. You can't beat that. There has to be a certain clarity in that.

I want to think there must have been a certain clarity to all the preparations here at Lowell at the telescope's installation. That complex trusswork of the great barnlike interior of the dome seems to support, against the sky, the same clear, earnest and immediate expectations as those raised as actual barns above the prairie by straw-hatted gangs of Mennonites. The same thin hope, the same strained practicalities extending, drawn and crossed and stressed and fastened to the space to hold the thought—that same thought, surely; that same gaze toward that same possibility. As if it might be possible to take the expectation of the prairie, all the longing of that horizontal emptiness, and redirect it up like this, express it up, straight up and away like early Gothic architecture, maybe—all that shoring up and strug-gle toward such grace. It looks like pine, old ambered pine—the spidery trusswork and the curving bent-board paneling below. Josh shows us scientific scribblings on the woodwork here and there where information, in the dark and under difficult condi-tions, had to find the nearest surface—I can't make much out except to note the number for the color filter commonly used for Mars to bring out maximum detail. A number 25 red filter. Which is still the one you want for visual use. For contrast. Maybe for a certain depth of feeling. At the center of the dome the monumental, freshly gloss-gray-painted cast-iron pier is waiting for the telescope. Although it seems to me it might as happily receive some great bronze statue—Lowell, Slipher, Ga-lileo, sturdy Mennonite. Behold our space, our emptiness, our homely, barnlike struggle to contain it.

The great telescope itself, the Clark refractor, is in pieces—
gorgeous remachined and reconditioned polished brass and iron
and wooden pieces—all laid out in the machine shop and awaiting reassembly. Just inside a big bay door they've parked that
giant, raisable observation platform that presents him, in that
plank-braced kitchen chair in that old photo, to the instrument.
And here's the chair. Or one exactly like it—it turns out he may
have had another one or two braced up like that. Like this old
dusty, spindly kitchen chair with peeling paint. Sure, have a look
across the unimaginable gulf at the evaporated tracings of intelligence out there, a sort of diagram so vast and thin and finely
drawn it vanishes. Pull up a chair—just any old chair—and have
a look. But brace yourself. Be still.

★

NOW HERE'S THE PART I'M NOT SO SURE ABOUT. HOW MEANINGFUL OR
trivial. Or both—some insights seem to find their purchase at
the boundary. Next to nothing—yet compelling, more compelling even, scrawled along the curving wooden surface of the
question, in the dark and under difficult conditions. After we
get back to Dallas and I've entered all my notes into my little
pocket journal—undeveloped, disconnected notes with pictures
pasted in about all this: our time with Theodore; our stops at
Arcosanti, Lowell Observatory, Meteor Crater, and the ghostly
nearby ruins of the '40s–'50s H. H. Nininger American Meteorite Museum; then our trip to the Grand Canyon and that
imitation Puebloan watchtower built by Mary Colter in the
1930s on the very edge of the South Rim and provided with
these quite bizarre "reflectoscopes" (you must incline your head

above the blackened glass to get the dizzy, dark, inverted view); and finally back down through Sedona to attempt, among the magic vortex crystal shops, to see if aught remains of Harvey Nininger's second Meteorite Museum—getting all this scribbled down without much sense of how it wants to come together (I'll get to it) but determined that it should, that it should constitute, be made to constitute, some sort of evidence, I find I keep returning to a sort of gap, an emptiness, a silence at the center of that dome where Lowell spent his time describing Mars, a dead spot where, in spite of all I've tried to say, my own thoughts, pressed to figure out that clarity, that "thought" I think I sense, that I impute, just cancel out. I print some copies, larger copies, of my photographs and spread them out and note how much more like an actual dome it seems from inside—how the bracing springs away like flying buttresses from angled, butting surfaces to round it out, to trace a sort of floating inner hemisphere. If I just push these photographs around it ought to come to me. And after a while it does. Or something does.

Here's a photograph of Nancy at the end of our tour in the reading room of the Slipher Building—1916, residential quarters for administrative and scientific staff. It must be pretty much the way it was back then—old leather-upholstered mission oak, old brass refractor by the window, old framed photographs of scientific worthies along the walls, and, in a corner by itself where Nancy stands before it gazing into the soft Mars-colored light, an old floor lamp in that same mission/Stickley style atop whose tripod-footed post a six-sided Japanese lantern-like box now glows with views, six different amber-tinted views of Mars as big as dinner plates, as drawn by Percival Lowell, fully imagined with canals traced out, oases shaded in, and all identified in elegant, timeless roman and italic by those classical/mythological names that lend such learned weightiness to these imagined features. And so strangely all that strangeness introduced here to illuminate these comfortable quarters easily and naturally as light through Tiffany flowers. Place that photo on the left. And to the right of it a close-up of one face of the lamp that shows a view of the south pole with the polar cap withdrawn, which doesn't seem to appear in Lowell's books—or not the ones I have. But it's quite striking in the zoned and crisscrossed symmetry presented by the structure of the canals. Then next to that a shot straight up of the interior of the dome, the zoned and crisscrossed lacy structure of the trusswork. And that's it. Not to suggest that Martian structures find their model in this trusswork—earlier drawings, after all, were made under different circumstances. And yet there is something here. Some sort of convergence. It's so close. Even the color. Ponderosa pine, says Kevin Schindler, outreach manager here for twenty years, as kind and patient as his colleague. They threw it up in a pretty big hurry to get it ready for the favorable opposition of 1896. Not even expecting it to be permanent. So you sense a sort of thoughtlessness—that "thought" that comes through thoughtlessness, that gesture that emerges on its own—in that gang of workers from the town who'd never built a thing like this before; so instinct must have guided them to draw it out like this, describe the space, invent the structure of this hollow inner eye (one thinks of the retinal theory of Lowell's Venusian markings). And it really is like drawing, how they've sketched it out, relieved it from exterior constraints, with strutting, curving two-by-twelves and two-by-sixes. It remains to give these structural elements classical names, I guess. To generalize what's going on. To formalize the deeper structure represented—to the point, and here's the point: It may be trivial to say this is the way we structure things. This is the diagram, sweet diagram, the thinnest vellum overlay we place upon the world, upon the emptiness we feel.

★

I HAVE NO FEELINGS FOR METEOR CRATER. AS IT TURNS OUT. NOT-withstanding the extraordinary drama of it here in the dead-flat middle of the northern Arizona desert, framed by distant peaks and low, blue ridges. Can't make sense of it. Can't fathom it somehow. The most spectacularly explicit impact feature in the world, at nearly a mile across, and fresh enough to demonstrate the actual plunge and splatter of the blast, still, after fifty thousand years. What's there to say or think about it? *Holy moly* comes to mind. I take some photos out of a sense of obligation but the only one I paste into my journal is a shot of a random patch of crater wall through one of the gimballed public telescopes they've set up on the rim. It's like you're peering through a wrapping-paper tube. A circular glimpse of overexposure. Slightly darkened along one side because off-center—so a gibbous overexposure like a planetary disk with intermingled watery blues and cloudy whites just like a world afloat in the dark. An earth. If you didn't know, you'd say that's what it is. A shot of the earth, a very cloudy, slightly unfamiliar earth—it's hard to make it look like anything else—from space. A world like ours. It's just an accident, of course. The blue a product of the intervening haze. There's nothing revelatory, surely. There's no way to make it meaningful. Suggest, say, that the impact sort of stuttered other planetary notions out of the ground. Or that it acted like an alchemist's mortar and pestle to refine from rude ingredients some universal tendency, some essence of the world precipitated to the surface here. Detectable obliquely with the proper instrumentation. That's too easy. Or too complicated. Certainly too glib. And, after all, what's *not* detectable with the proper instrumentation? Still, it goes into the journal. It's so beautiful.

About five miles away, back down the road from Meteor Crater to the highway, on a forbidden bleached and crumbling stretch of old Route 66, are the Tintagel-like ruins of Nininger's American Meteorite Museum. He was here for seven years— from '46 to '53, until the interstate passed him by—in this peculiar former curio shop and Meteor Crater "observatory" built of local sandstone in the 1930s. What a curious situation—to have aligned himself out here along "the Mother Road" with all those gaudy institutions advertising relics, reptiles, mummified desert mysteries. I imagine it must have seemed a sixteenth-century sort of struggle to present the scientific as distinct from so much rumor, superstition, and sensation.

I remember roadside mysteries. For the most part in a general sort of way, a sense that, traveling those old routes before the interstate passed things by, you actually penetrated something, moved along some deep incision (like an alley, I suppose) that laid things open—our internals, our subconscious—to amazed and sometimes horrified inspection. One exhibit I recall in some detail—in some dark curio shop somewhere; it might have been Route 66 but I suspect old Highway 80, nearer home; I was too young, at eight or so, to have a clear idea of distances; when we were on the road we might be anywhere—but anyway, we'd stopped, I think toward evening, and I found myself astonished and confused and possibly saddened by a mermaid in a jar. She was not pickled; rather mummified, it seemed. About the size of a small monkey, dry and shrunken. It said "Mermaid" on the jar. If there was further information, I've forgotten. It could only have made it worse—to have specifics as to where and when and how this could have happened. Such a shimmery, dreamy notion dragged to the surface and collapsed into a thing like this, so ugly one assumed it must be real. Why have it, otherwise? The question has to do less with reality than the value of such things, exalted notions. Oh well, sure, if you mean *that,* then there *are* mermaids. Santa Claus and God as well—but not the way you like to think. I thought it best to rejoin my parents and not mention it. Just keep it to myself. Of course much later I would come to understand that it was a standard sort of taxidermic fake involving mismatched (fish and mammal) parts; or maybe one of those reconstructed, dried, and varnished rays called "Jenny Hanivers" (for reasons not entirely clear) beloved of Dutch fishermen and sailors, who would make them, cut and fold them into mermaids, dragons, angels. Even angels. Why not go ahead and make it be an angel? One imagines some old sailor on the docks of Rotterdam thinking, cutting, folding this poor creature, its reality, the terrible and marvelous compliance of reality, available if fresh enough to bend, distort—the lapping of the ocean right there under him—into whatever dreamy, holy, fearful thing you like. If there were angels, falling angels, say, might they not likely fall into the ocean, tend to wash up on the beach and look like this? Not like you thought. Nor like they were, perhaps. But, still, a core, a remnant. Mundane residue. Suggesting that from which they must have come. Don't you imagine? That oblique and rudimentary apprehension. First the misinterpretation—something glimpsed out of the corner of your eye. And then it's there. Whole worlds emerge. In the Bishop Museum on the island of Oahu, from the old stone-tesserae floor in which it is embedded, there emerges—or emerged at least when I was there about thirty years ago—a gray stone fish god someone dug up as instructed in his dream. As I recall it's pretty massive—maybe five feet tall and half a ton, perhaps, of some dense gray volcanic stone. Basalt of some sort sheared from a larger mass, you'd think, to get that strain, that bend you see sometimes on struck flint blades. That tension as from the force of separation, revelation caught there in it, in the hollow, vaguely anthropomorphic leaning forward of it toward the eye that saw it looking back and knew the way to bring that out, encourage what inhered, peck out the empty eyes, the gaping, tragic Greek-theatrical mouth, the awful self-surprise and terror of it. What a thing for some poor haunted fisherman to pull out of the ground, out of his dream. In 1885, according to the note I wrote on my little drawing of it. On Kawaihae, Kohala, Hawaii, in the middle of the night.

So here was Nininger, former teacher of biology at a small midwestern college, man of reason, foremost expert in and principal founder of the infant field of meteoritics, having failed to arrange to place his vast collection in a museum on the actual rim of the crater and so retreated to this weird stone former curio shop five miles away aligned with all that lesser stuff, that failure of the mind, that great transcontinental side show. He had nothing to do with that, regretted all that ghastly signage along the highway. Yet the traffic he depended on was traffic for the other, for the relics and the trinkets and the mysteries of the desert. It would all have seemed a mystery, I suspect. Back in the day. To drive Route 66, especially in the summer without air-conditioning, trying to stay awake, your windows open, kids asleep in the back. And every now and then these apparitions, marvels looming—see the mermaid, see the fish god, see "The Mystery Thing of the Desert"—like you're traveling through a dream. And I imagine all that ignorance and wonder flowed right through him. Paid its money. Took a look and drove away. The building leaked. The old mud mortar stained the walls. The science—the meteoritics—probably seemed to blur a little in such circumstances. Certainly to the various institutions that consistently refused to grant him funding it seemed compromised, diffused somewhat, arising from and catering to the popular stream of mind that came away with souvenirs: these rather tacky little pamphlets with sensational cover graphics of a streaking cartoon comet with a meteoric fragment (actually oxide) pasted into a little round window at its nucleus; real specimens of Meteor Crater "irons" made into jewelry. It gets well above one hundred in the summer in that part of Arizona. And without electrical power you'd expect the doors and windows to be open. You'd expect the dust to drift right through, the time of day as well, as natural light was all they had except for lanterns. How exposed they were. Uncloistered, uncredentialed, and unfunded. And so easily, maybe naturally, falling into association with the terrible and marvelous compliance of reality along that stretch of road. That what they had to show and tell was true did not disqualify it.

Twenty-five-cent admission, fifteen cents for kids—so get them up and drag them in, all sweaty, squinty, half-awake, to hear, from Nininger himself most likely, how the world lies open. How the sky falls in upon us all the time. Behold the evidence—the marvelous and, to a child of course, uneasy evidence up to the size of boulders. Not to mention, not to contemplate, the mile-wide crater five miles up the road. How critical, then, to come away with one of those pamphlets with the comet and that bit of actual meteoric oxide on the cover. Just to have it, touch that little rusty fragment. Like some ancient saintly relic, a protection, inoculation (What are the odds that anything could really happen while you hold it?) on that long and hot and terribly open road, however far you have to go, against whatever looms, descends.

The ruins really do seem blasted. Vastly older than they are. There was a fire, I'm told, that caused the main collapse. With such a picturesque result. You think, again, My goodness, how exposed they were. Or, in the dark Romantic nineteenth-century spirit of such picturesqueness, How exposed we are. How truly perilous the gap between the flat red earth and pale blue sky that children's paintings sometimes make explicit.

It's been fenced off though. A gate across that remnant of the highway with emphatic black and yellow "No Trespassing" signs on posts and one on the gate itself. And way out there across the scrub in that white, hazy space between the earth and sky, the place where we would like to go. An appeal at the RV park nearby (at the suggestion of the staff at Meteor Crater) does the trick. A call is made. An invocation of my literary mission. And we're in. So through the gate (between the rails) and maybe a half mile down the crumbly path that makes us wonder that it ever could have been "the Mother Road." The great transnational cultural incision. Healed to a fading scar out here. No more than an intermittent trace of the old white line.

The "picturesque," back when it meant more than it usually means today, contained a sense of the sublime, whose meaning also has decayed. "Sublime," especially as descriptive of those lofty, craggy, overpowering ruin-dotted landscapes so appealing to Romantics of the late eighteenth and early nineteenth centuries, sought to express a certain horror that arose, on contemplation of the magnitude of Nature, at that point where notions of beauty, conventional order, seemed to fail. It was, for a while, a mark of cultural and spiritual distinction, like the hajj, to have made the journey—to the Lake District, the Alps—to place oneself before such wild upliftings, terrible inflections and distortions of the earth as to induce a sort of thrill of personal frailty and precariousness. Eventually enlisted, nevertheless, into the popular aesthetic—to the beautiful what once had seemed to threaten it. A strategy that carries through to modern art, at times becoming almost a defining characteristic.

As we make our way out to it, it's as if all that sublime, Romantic, mountainous topography, where picturesque tradition still inclines us to imagine such a ruin, had eroded, blown away as inessential. As a mere exhilaration, a distraction from the truer, thinner, flatter, scarier question. Here is something left of that Romantic precipice where balances the soul. Although de-

flated and refined and undramatic. Not at all the way we probably like to think.

The usual photograph of Nininger is posed. He wears a tie
and holds a magnifying glass above a meteorite. There's little to
be seen that way—it's mostly just the gesture, the idea of objec-
tivity. Of scientific rigor. There's a need to hold himself away
like that. A variation—in a photo in his autobiography, *Find a
Falling Star* (whose title always makes me wince)—shows him in
lecture mode at the Route 66 museum. Standing next to him a
young girl in a straw hat gazes up at his remarks made with the
aid of a wooden pointer which extends across the girl to rest
upon a heavy specimen her father (one assumes) presents. The
pointer isn't needed. He could reach. He wears a tie. He needs
to demonstrate a certain formal distance. In this case about a
foot and a half, I'd say. Look how established, poised he is in this
uncertain space. Outside the dust is blowing, daylight gathering
or departing. The horizon faded out to a kind of empty, dusty
white presumably left by the collapse of all that self-exalting,
wild, ecstatic, picturesque topography. He knows, at this point,
more than anyone else about all this. About the chemistry of
meteorites, their structure and the unsuspected frequency. He
knows about it clearly, scientifically. From time to time would
even publish scientific papers. Yet his pose seems so compensa-
tory. Studiously counter to some deeper popular impulse to
present it all sensationally, to feed it into the stream of common
terrors and amazements. How bizarre, how like a fun house
must have been those late appointments that required a tour by
lantern light. My goodness, what a ruin. It's the ruin of a structure built on instinct. You don't get this sort of ruin anymore.

This sort of sad, majestic, incremental falling apart requires to act upon a certain structural consistency. A uniform intention/intuition incrementally expressed—the hoist and slap and scrape of mud and rock—repeated till it's done. Throughout, the same—from ground to tower. There's a tower at one end. That seems to have been the "observatory." Just like Jericho's. So, crumbling just like Jericho.

When I was vaguely fading out of graduate school in English, I would sometimes skip my classes to attend those of a friend in archaeology. My favorite was about the Neolithic of the Middle East. And one particular lecture having to do with excavations at the ancient site of Jericho excited me immensely. The professor was one of those who could unsquint from all the narrow archaeological detail to gaze into that dusty, wide-eyed moment thousands of years before the God of Abraham condensed out of whatever was floating around out there before such things as pottery or proper agriculture, where arose in that vast emptiness for reasons not entirely clear these fifteen-foot stone walls with this great thirty-foot stone tower on one side. Can you imagine walking out of the flat and endless Neolithic toward a thing like that with sunrise gleaming off its limestone face? What in the world was being defended or confronted or addressed? No one quite knows—or not, at least, with any certainty. Suggestions that the tower is positioned along the wall to intercept the advancing shadow (and, therefore, those powers resident in shadow) of a mountain on the evening of the summer solstice seem a little fanciful. And yet the straight stone stairs within the tower do appear to rise toward the mountain and align, as if intended, with the sunset on that day. Which makes for a pretty good story of course. And a nice computer simulation, which the authors of the paper have provided as an oddly sinister graphic. In effect they've built a model that pre-dates Monopoly houses by at least ten thousand years and slowly, carefully, bent their desk lamp down toward sunset on that longest day of the year in the Jordan Valley. There's a double time-lapse sequence running vertically down the page. At left, the long view of the mountain—Quruntul, not very big as mountains go but where the Devil will tempt Jesus in about eight thousand years and rather ominous here, its eastern flank in shadow—and the town about a mile away, set out in a bright rectangular frame for emphasis. At right a schematic close-up of the reconstructed tower, wall, and various smaller structures casting shadows with the date, June 21, and time for each pair—long shot/close-up—marked in red. The mountain's shadow, on the left, runs like a mudslide toward the town in five-minute increments. The simulation makes it look like something rather worse than night is coming. There's a drama, a forensic sort of focus to this kind of presentation. Yet who knows what Neolithic night was like? Perhaps a sense of that has leaked into the simulated moment. Inadvertently. A simulated sense of how it felt. Between the first pair (17:50) and the second (17:55) a point, a sort of pseudopod, of shadow, in the long shot, has extended out across the plain directly toward the town. And for the next five double frames it goes like that—a cinematic back-and-forth between the close-up, where it all seems fine, just evening, simple shadows that in thousands of years will be the simple shadows of Monopoly houses, ordinary neighborhoods, while on the left the deeper and, who knows, perhaps eternal, Neolithic darkness creeps.

And then at 18:25 (Oh, Jericho! Oh, white wall of Spain!) it all goes dark.

We wander about for a while in the ruins. Try to imagine how it was. You get the feeling—though the fire came many years after—that they left here just in time. H.H. and Addie, his wife, who always looks the same—a little grim, a little older than her husband. There's a shot of them together in his autobiography. Here he's more relaxed. No tie. No magnifying glass. He's sitting outside in a folding chair at a white-cloth-covered table where a couple of hundred tektites (glassy, oddly sculpted stones that are thought to represent the splatter from large meteoric impacts) have been sorted. He still grasps one in his right hand as he looks up at the camera. Addie's standing, in a white blouse and a print skirt, leaning in as if to fit into the frame. It is the simplest and most ordinary moment. It should be the daily harvest of pecans or figs. No mystery. No impingement from beyond. A simple snapshot at a simple family gathering in the backyard—other white-cloth-covered tables will have jugs of tea, potato salad. Look how close they are to this—no protocol, no distance. How composed and calm within this understanding. We're exposed—the simple, ordinary world exposed—in ways we hardly know. He would go knock on farmhouse doors to ask what might have been plowed up. Might have been tossed out by the fence, become a doorstop. He would go among the cotton hoers, right out into the fields to show them what they ought to look for. The exposure that was clearest to our simplest state of mind.

This place is shattered. Broken plates of pink-red sandstone scattered everywhere. I hold one out to Nancy. She's a painter. I am always importuning for a drawing: "You should draw on this." But she already has. She takes a jagged, palm-sized tablet from her bag and there's a ghostly charcoal outline of the ruin. Ghostly prehistoric petrograph of ghostly ruined future. Pretty spooky.

There's a bathtub full of rubble. There's a big white-sprayed graffito of a heart below "Forever" and enclosing "Greg loves Debi." There's a raven's nest (I'm guessing—massive accumulation of sticks) in what must once have been a window in the tower. A few yards away, downslope, a couple of rusting wrecks—a 1958 (I think) Impala and a 1970s Oldsmobile on whose flank has been painted "Merry Christmas." It's all ruined. Past and future. Nancy finds a rusty lunch box on the ground inside the structure. It's a schoolchild's cartoon Route 66–themed lunch box with an anthropomorphic sports car from some animated movie smiling out from under a shield-shaped Route 66 sign and a banner at the top that reads, "The Mother Road." Good Lord. It seems too much. We take a photograph and leave it. Then she's standing by a broken-out stone window, nothing there but empty distance—scrub and haze and deepening blue— and yet she beckons, quite excited. "Get a picture, please." She points. A tiny bee floats in that empty, ruined space. It's absolutely still. It holds that space in place the way some hovering insects do as if obedient to, in reference to, some universal center. I can't see it in my camera. "Higher, up, up, get it, please." She wants that bee. She's almost frantic. There. I show her. Zoom it in. And there it is—in focus even, perfectly still within the empty, ruined window of the Meteorite Museum on the ruins of the road through our subconscious, in the middle of the world and on and on as far as you like, on out as far as there are references. A dream of perfect stillness. I believe I've never seen her quite so happy.

*

I SHOULD BACK UP HERE. THE NIGHT BEFORE WE LEFT FOR ARCOSANTI— and our philosophical survey or whatever this is—we stayed in a pretty nice hotel in Tempe. I had time to get set up—to commandeer the desk and swivel chair, lay out my pad and printouts—and attempt to make some sense of things. Or postulate some sense that might be made—you never know how things will go. But anyway, it seemed to me if there was going to be a way to think my way into all this (whatever this is) it might, somehow, be through the Claude glass, that once-fashionable device of high Romantic sensibility that inspired those black "reflectoscopes" installed by Mary Colter at her watchtower on the rim of the Grand Canyon. Do you know about the Claude glass? It's an instrument designed to have you turn away from that you wish to study. A device precisely for averted vision. Though in a worldly rather than astronomical sense. I had printed out a page from the U.K. National Trust Collections showing a full-length portrait, attributed to Edward Alcock (fl. 1757–1778), of Sophia Anne Delaval, second daughter of John, Lord Delaval, "holding a Claude glass to the landscape." It belongs to a set depicting all four sisters—each in that plinth-and-drapery neoclassical style, each with some personal totem (peahen, floral watercolor, dog), and with a misty landscape opening behind, to which Sophia holds, face out to us, a Claude glass in a gold frame. Nancy thinks there's something sad and very human showing through the rather stolid, formulaic presentation of this woman all got up in the silken grandeur of the era. And in fact, as I researched, hers does appear to have been a troubled life with disagreeable husbands, opium debts. Her Claude glass seems to be a lens, for you can see, reduced, the distant landscape in it. But I think—and Nancy agrees—this must be license, since the Claude glass was (as commonly understood) a tinted, slightly convex mirror carried about by late-eighteenth- and early-nineteenth-century tourists who, so curiously, found the sublimity of Nature more acceptable, more picturesque, as rendered less majestic in these optical devices—those exhilarating prospects more admired the more compressed, the more composed in tidy, golden-toned reflections, as it were, of the seventeenth-century landscape style of Claude Lorrain. And were it a simple lens, the image would be inverted, which it's not. It is as if the view were fixed upon the glass—in anticipation of photography. As if she were displaying, in that golden frame, her own sad, distant gaze. I'm thinking now, how like the photographs of Nininger—the posed ones with the magnifying glass. The sort of thing you tend to want to make too much of. Still, there's something. Surely. Having come this far. To come upon her, unlike Dee and Lowell and Nininger, gazing out at us. No program. Just the gaze. The sad and human one that Nancy feels emerges from her portrait and the one she holds, presumably internal and reflected in her mirror. There is no investigation. There's no intercession, even, taking place. She looks at us, holds out the image in the instrument as if to say, Well, here you are. At last. So far from every natural moment, so got up, so still, so captured in the formalism. What you have at last is still that distance. That great emptiness. That surface of the earth. This or another. Think of Oumarou again at the end of Anna Badkhen's book, transhumant patriarch so sad on his plastic sheet—as artificial, as constraining, as her silk—becoming briefly sedentary in his sadness (maybe sadness is a sedentary thing), so many children, cattle, lost. So far to go.

All I could think, though, at the time was how her mirror—image fixed and turned to us—seemed like a hole punched through the picture into something real, removed. And how the Claude glass might have served the "picturesque" in ways more startling and bewildering than we know.

★

ABOUT A YEAR AGO WE FOUND OURSELVES AT THE WATCHTOWER ON the edge of the Grand Canyon. I had written about the Claude glass years before and was aware of the "reflectoscopes." So why, on that occasion, I ignored them I can't say. Perhaps the crowd. Or a sort of snobbishness on my part—those black mirrors weren't Claude glasses; they were flat. The signage, too, was irritating in attributing the invention of the optical device to the painter for whom, a century after as his landscapes were discovered to reflect the current picturesque aesthetic, it was named. In any case I came to realize that I'd missed my chance at something. So we're back. It's pretty early. Not too crowded on the observation terrace—where, at intervals, are set into the circular sandstone parapet a number (five, I think) of those black mirrors, each contained within a reddish-brown-painted wooden box with a slot in the top to look through. And the boxes, you can see, slip in and out of their positions in the wall (for regular cleaning, I suppose) along pairs of rails carved out of splitting weathered logs. As if the whole peculiar arrangement were intended to seem a natural component of this imitation Puebloan construction. As if we were to pretend that the Ancients used such things. To guide in ancient spaceships, say. Communicate with spirits. It requires that you approach the box, lean over and peer through the slot, risk losing your glasses, perched on your head, to the depths in sacrificial exchange, perhaps, for the deeper, visionary glimpse of the canyon somewhat dimmed and upside down. Imagine ancient iridescing piles of spectacles like bones down there somewhere. Beats me. Though Nancy notes that the colors seem enhanced. I don't quite get it. All this effort. Like those telescopes provided here and there along the rim of Meteor Crater in response to some sort of urge, I guess, to scrutinize the emptiness. These wild and unexpected sorts of emptiness especially. Behold, apply your magnifying glass, where everything you take for granted falls away. I may have glanced away before, when we were here, the way a dog will turn away from its reflection. Nope, not me. I don't contain that possibility. That gap. That sad and distant sense of meaning gazing back upon itself. I'm just a dog. So what's for lunch?

We stop in Flagstaff at a little bar and grill we liked before. Then back toward Tempe through Sedona where, from '53 to '60, Nininger had his second Meteorite Museum in a blocky little building he constructed on the highway. I am hoping something's left of it as well. But driving into town, it's Disneyland—all goofy "vortex" crystal shops and ice-cream shops and get-your-picture-taken-all-dressed-up-like-famous-outlaws. I'm discouraged. We've a copy of a postcard photo of it. Although Nininger never liked the old stone building near the crater, he appears to have memorialized it here in brick and concrete block, with an Art Deco–ish ornamental tower at one end. I'm not sure why I'm so concerned to find a remnant. We inquire among the older bearded and ponytailed merchants, wander down to the chamber of commerce office. Show the picture—shakes of heads and looks of sympathy as for a missing loved one, but no luck. Then Nancy, noticing that the mountains in the background of the picture are the same ones we can see from here, just shifted, parallactically displaced, bids me return the way we came—across the street, back down the sidewalk, through the tourists, past the crystal shops and cowboy shops and Indian shops as near and distant peaks and knobby mesas start to slip into a meaningful relation. And then there it is. My God, I love this woman. It's right there across the two-lane blacktop highway. Much made over and appended to a small hotel whose Styrofoam-adobe style it shares. But still that little Deco tower poking up. That's it. No question. It's the perfect time of day—the light, the shadows. It remains to get the angle. I slip down the dirt embankment from the elevated sidewalk, find myself astride a big protruding rock—the same one surely, it becomes clear through the camera, that supported the photographer of that postcard image sixty years ago—to take the very same shot. It all shifts into phase. The road, the mountains, and the fading afternoon—all of those fading afternoons—achieve this limited agreement, this coincidence like squinting through the viewer on an old range-finder camera trying to get the doubled image to converge upon itself, to get to focus. Seems to me there'd be this bright one and this dim one—it's been years—a double image of your loved one, say, so you would have to turn the dial on the lens until they came together. Bright and dim combine, the gap is closed, and there she is. And there you are.

★

BACK HOME I'M ENTERING MY NOTES INTO MY JOURNAL, PASTING two-by-three-inch copies of my photos in, not trying, as I've said, to make much sense of it—not having even formed the question yet about the "silence" at the center of the dome at Lowell Observatory. Just trying to get it down before I start to misremember, reinterpret. There is a curious satisfaction pasting photos in among the text like this. As if the words—my messy scrawl perhaps especially—were like leaves and dust blown in through open windows. You can shuffle around in the leaves however you like. Make little paths and piles. But then you pause and find yourself just gazing out the window. Look what happens here. With postage stamp–sized copies of the old and current Meteorite Museum buildings pasted side by side. The postcard one on the left and the one I took on the right, sixty years or so between. The angle, light, and shadows— everything is perfect. And I see now that they make a perfect stereoscopic pair. Except what separates them, what is to be reconciled, is history, not space. So that would make—what? An histereoscopic pair? Without a viewer, there are two ways you can do this. You can cross your eyes to overlap the images— which feels a little forced, somehow mechanical. Or you can just de-focus as if you were really gazing out a window at those mountains in the distance. As if that were really distance. The same distance sixty years ago as now. Which should be obvious, of course, but seems a little strange to say. You just relax. You let it go. It's like a sigh when you release your gaze like that. You feel it go as air comes in. As these two photographs converge it's like the window sliding open. Or more open. You don't get that sudden locking into place as with a simple, spatial stereoscopic image. There's too much to bring together—all that overlapping distance, all those fading afternoons. But you can tell. As with averted vision—oh, there's something. Not exactly depth, but something like that. Something sort of perpendicular to that. The rutted dirt and golden light of the postcard photo drift across into the brighter flat-blue present. What was present. Both are true. Indifferent. Joined in that coherent sort of blur. Can that be true? As true as depth? Can the confusion be essential information? The refusal to resolve, itself resolve into the thing? What is the thing? In Anna Badkhen's *Walking with Abel,* the Fulani, in a sense, become their cattle. And their cattle, clouds of dust. They can identify the herd, and thus the herdsman, by the dust. By his dispersal. Look what happens. Anna sees them as dispersed in all directions—"across eras . . . driving true and phantom herds." A blur of brighter ones and dimmer ones. They move within this dusty cloud of music that emerges from the cellphones they suspend from their necks or boom boxes "decorated with small mirrors, like disco balls" strapped to their chests—all mingling strangely with their "yips and ululations" in this vast attenuation into that imponderable distance like their breath drawn out, their hearts drawn out. It's thrilling—must be thrilling, the coherence of the blur. Try to imagine, from some distant elevation, watching all this moving out across the ancient scrubby surface of the earth to ancient boom box strains of Kim Carnes singing "Bette Davis Eyes."

8

I AM PUZZLED BY THE MOURNFULNESS OF CITIES. I SUPPOSE I MEAN American cities mostly—dense and vertical and relatively sudden. All piled up in fullest possible distinction from surroundings, from our flat and grassy origins, the migratory blur from which the self, itself, would seem to have emerged into the emptiness, the kindergarten-landscape gap between the earth and sky. I'm puzzled, especially, by what seems to me the ease of it, the automatic, fundamental, even corny quality of mournfulness in cities, so built into us, so preadapted for somehow, that even camped out there on the savannah, long before we dreamed of cities, I imagine we should probably have had a premonition, dreamed the sound of lonely saxophones on fire escapes. What's mourned is hard to say. Not that the mourner needs to know. It seems so basic. One refers to certain Edward Hopper paintings—

people gazing out of windows right at sunset or late at night. They've no idea. I don't suppose that sort of gaze is even possible except within the city. You can hear the lonely saxophone-on-fire-escape (in principle, the instrument may vary) cry through Gershwin. Aaron Copland. You remember Sonny Rollins on the bridge (the structure varies too, of course). So what in the world is that about? That there should be a characteristic thread of melody, a certain sort of mood to sound its way through all that lofty, sooty jumble to convey so clear and, as it seems, eternal a sense of loss and resignation. How in the world do you get eternal out of saxophone and fire escape? It doesn't make much sense. That it should get to you—to me at least—more sharply, deeply, sadly than the ancient, naturally mournful, not to say eternal, sound of breath through reed or bamboo flute.

Not too many years ago as I began to wonder about the mournfulness of cities—its expression in this way—I brought a recording of Aaron Copland's *Quiet City* concert piece to my (then) girlfriend Nancy's house on a chilly winter evening. She had friends or family staying, so we slept in the front bedroom which, because of its exposure or some problem with the heater, was quite cold. So I remember all the quilts and blankets and huddling up together as if desperate in some Lower East Side tenement and listening to this music break our hearts about ourselves, our struggling immigrant immersion and confusion in this terrible complexity. The lonely verticality of life. And why should sadness sound so sweet? I guess the sweetness is the resignation part.

I'd like to set up an experiment to chart the sadness—try to find out where it comes from, where it goes—to trace it, in that melody (whichever variation) as it threads across Manhattan from the Lower East Side straight across the river, more or less west, into the suburbs of New Jersey and whatever lies beyond. This would require, I'm guessing, maybe a hundred saxophonists stationed along the route on tops of buildings, water towers, farther out on people's porches (with permission), empty parking lots, at intervals determined by the limits of their mutual audibility under variable conditions in the middle of the night, so each would strain a bit to pick it up and pass it on in step until they're going all at once and all strung out along this fraying thread of melody for hours, with relievers in reserve. There's bound to be some drifting in and out of phase, attenuation of the tempo, of the sadness for that matter, of the waveform, what I think of as the waveform of the whole thing as it comes across the river losing amplitude and sharpness, rounding, flattening and diffusing into neighborhoods where maybe it just sort of washes over people staying up to hear it or, awakened, wondering what is that out there so faint and faintly echoed, faintly sad but not so sad that you can't close your eyes again and drift right back to sleep.

It isn't possible to hear it all at once. You have to track the propagation. All those saxophones receiving and repeating and coordinating, maybe, for an interval or two before the melody escapes itself to separate into these brief, discrete, coherent moments out of sync with one another, coming and going, reconnecting, fading out and in again along the line in ways that someone from an upper-story window at a distance might be able to appreciate, able to pick up, who knows, ten or twenty instruments way out there faintly gathering, shifting in and out of phase along a one- or two-mile stretch. And I imagine it would be all up and down like that—that long, sad train of thought disintegrating, recomposing here and there all night in waves and waves of waves until the players, one by one, begin to give it up toward dawn like crickets gradually flickering out.

In order to chart the whole thing as intended, though, we will need a car, someone to drive it slowly along the route with the windows down while someone else—me, I suppose—deflects a pen along some sort of moving scroll, perhaps a foot wide and a hundred feet long, that has been prepared with a single complex line of reference along the top, a kind of open silhouette, a structural cross section through the route, with key points noted, from the seismic verticalities of Manhattan through the quieter inflections of New Jersey and those ancient tract-house neighborhoods and finally going flat (as I imagine, having no idea what's out there) into what? Savannah, maybe? Or some open field with the final saxophonist all alone out there in the grass.

So, as this scroll is turned within its windowed box on a pair of rollers—either motorized and GPS-controlled or simply cranked by someone trained to keep it all coordinated—I attempt to get myself into a Zen-like state of mind and let my deeper instincts twitch the pen, a red one, down or up to chart the mournfulness, its zigzag fluctuations in that thin melodic line as followed out into the night. Of course, there's nothing scientific involved. No rigor here at all. It's more like dowsing. I'll be predisposed to chart my expectation—which is that the overall profile of the sadness will reflect (as a mirror image) that of the city as it tails off into Jersey and the suburbs and beyond.

But who knows? There might be anomalous fluctuations. I might find myself sufficiently detached and unself-conscious in the process, weirdly neutral in the weirdness of the thing, that I allow my hand to twitch in unexpected ways at unexpected thumpings of my heart, the red line suddenly reversing, say, toward joy, then spiking down again, and wildly back and forth at certain places. Alleys, vacant lots—the intermittent reassertion of that flat and grassy emptiness where joy and sorrow first arose and, still, may tend to flip-flop, switch polarities. Though, surely, it's inevitable that sadness and its reference, as we travel farther west, will flatten out, go parallel and possibly merge.

What have we got, then, when it's done? When we roll it out? A line of history, I think. I'd like to think. From left to right, from west to east, from out in the flatlands, in the field with that last saxophone where the lines of the world and our feelings about it probably coincide, back there before the Neolithic; on up into those New Jersey tract-house neighborhoods where the lines diverge and consciousness of a sad and workmanlike sort arises faintly in the sedentary morning, every morning, people waking up into it just like history; up the line, the double line now, toward increasing complication and divergence, over the river (under the river—haven't figured that part out) into those terribly vertical regions where we find ourselves with saxophones on fire escapes, in Edward Hopper paintings, lost, heartbroken, fully distinct, alone at last.

*

ANNA BADKHEN TOLD ME ABOUT A SAXOPHONE PLAYER WHO SOME-times liked to practice in the West Philadelphia graveyard where she liked to go to be by herself and read. She'd hear him out there now and then standing next to his car and honking away. You'd think how sweet and strange and sad, of course, but Anna says he wasn't very good and, besides, whenever he'd make a mistake he'd simply lose it. Just go crazy. Cursing loudly and kicking his car. And he would make a lot of mistakes. Which must have made it hard to read. So, if not sweet, we're left with strange and sad. And a sense that it must mean something more than crazy. What directed him, I wonder? Toward so painful a production of it—driving to the cemetery, practicing so poorly, cursing and screaming and kicking his car. Again and again. Did he expect, each time, to find that he had improved? Or might the cursing and the kicking have been understood to be an unavoidable, even essential, part of the concert—best performed among the dead? Each struggling passage ending awkwardly and furiously and sadly with no sweetness in the sadness—none of that resignation here. No going gentle.

I don't think Anna ever mentioned what it was he tried to play. My sense is that it never really quite resolved. Nor did he seem to be attending a particular grave or anything like that. So, no clues there. He'd just drive in and park and stand by his car and get into this struggle. Far from the lofty, mournful reflections of the fire escape. As if descended, maybe, into this Orphic situation at the bottom end of things. Twice Anna passed him, thanked him for playing, and embarrassed him, she thinks. He wasn't there for her, of course. I doubt he knew what he was there for. I imagine myth and ritual are mindless in this way. It all just happens. One is drawn into this moment. Yanked into some deep significance. And generally released. But sometimes not. Sometimes entangled and perpetuated. What's to be per-petuated here? This poor guy's caught between the living and the dead, unable, quite, to find the tune. How does his day begin, do you think? In some apartment somewhere, in some simple room with simple windows to look out of? Kitchen table. Cup of coffee. Laundry tossed into a corner by the bed. As simple as that. As easy and unresolved as that. Why should it seem so unresolved? The sun comes up and there you are. You have your duty to perform. To engage the struggle in this mythic way for all of us. You come into the city and you go among the dead and screw it up and kick the car for us perpetually. And who knows, after centuries, told and retold over and over, what it means?

9

AMONG MY SCRIBBLY JOURNAL PAGES FROM OUR THREE-DAY STAY IN the Arcosanti Sky Suite, there's a scribbly ballpoint sketch of the view along a little path below our quarters. Why a sketch—and a poor one—rather than a photograph is hard to say. Perhaps to say I mean it. As Nancy says, the pencil moves "as if it's on the thing itself. It brings it into you." Well, not as strong as that with me, of course. But something like that, maybe. It just struck me one day coming up that path of intermittent concrete pavers in the grass between the sloping concrete wall to my left and the falling away of the hillside on my right and, straight ahead among the shrubbery, a tree, that I was looking into the past. My past, I guess, but past in general in a way. Who knows what circuits short when things like this occur. Here are my notes on the facing page:

Why does this view, this path along the side of one of the south-facing residences, just below the "Sky Suite," send me back a hundred years? To distant childhood? A glimpse as if from inside myself (as I have had infrequently before)—as if it brings the whole (whatever counts as whole) past with it. And a characteristic exhilaration—an absolute certainty attending it.

And on the right this doodle. As if one might render pastness with a hand sufficiently careless or inept. As if the truth might somehow drift into the scribble-scrabble of it and get caught in there. Entangled.

So, I'm walking back to the Sky Suite in the blazing afternoon and, just like that, I seem to come upon the past. It seems to concentrate up there where the path turns left by the tree and the view of the hills beyond. There is no sense of stunned recovery of some particular moment lost till now. No obvious trigger. Though of course one has to wonder what is going on subconsciously. And even how pathology might figure in. I am not feeling altogether well. And three and a half months hence I'll have a heart attack. They'll fix me up. I'll be okay. But now I think about de Chirico recovering from severe intestinal illness in a Florentine piazza back in 1910 or thereabouts—how, in his weakened state, in the autumn light, the ancient city square became a stage whereon could be observed, and then recorded in his "metaphysical" paintings, all laid open like an anatomy lesson, the mutual detachment of the arbitrary objects of the world. The silent, airless gulf between them as imponderable as that between the stars. You get a glimpse sometimes when things go wrong. The mechanism opens up a bit. And you see through it and beyond it in a way. All through my college years I drove a much-abused VW Beetle. Drove it pretty much into the ground—to the point where you really needed a tailwind to sustain the usual highway speed of fifty-five miles per hour. On its final voyage it carried me and three others to an air show in Fort Worth where the big attraction was the recently top-secret SR-71 spy plane guarded by a rope and an armed marine and rumored capable of speeds beyond Mach 3. I think we might have had a tailwind coming out, but going back it was a struggle for the first few miles. And then it's like we've topped the hill or something. Cars no longer seem to pass us quite so frequently. My friend Jim Lynch is driving. He loved driving. But he was a little crazy. Now we're doing sixty-five. So I lean up between the front seats and say, Hey, what's going on? Jim's hugging the wheel with this wild expression and a squint like he needs goggles. What the hell? He's got it floored. He's not about to back it off. He'll never get this chance again. We look around at one another. We're beginning to pass some cars. We're doing seventy-five and still accelerating. Holy crap. We've fallen silent. There are these aerodynamic sounds I've never heard before. Jim's locked onto the wheel. He is committed. We're at eighty. We are passing into a new regime. At any moment we might leave the road, go into hyperdrive with fenders, mirrors ripping off, the paint igniting, flaming away in flashes as we slip beyond the envelope of atmosphere and ordinary life. When you're that age, you've no idea. A thing like this might be your destiny. Then suddenly just silence. Not transonic, but the engine cutting out. No bang or clatter. Just the whistling of the wind through those little side vents like we're plummeting from altitude. Somehow we manage to coast it off the highway into a service station. Hardly even tap the brakes. We don't need gas. It just won't go. It's done. We call someone to pick us up. I sell the car to one of the guys who can use the parts. A week or so later I'm informed it threw a rod—though how so violent an event could have been so quiet is a mystery. Maybe a day or two after that, my friend comes over to present me with the camshaft. He regards it as a marvel. As suggesting both a further mystery—how my car could have run at all with cams so worn and misshapen—and a plausible explanation for its ultimate performance. Proper cams—that lift and close the engine valves controlling intake and exhaust—have tapered ovoid profiles much like that of a hen's egg. Mine have profiles more like that of a piece of popcorn. My friend speculates that somehow, at the end, these cams had worn into a shape that suddenly duplicated the function of what's called a "racing cam"—think of that deep, irregular gluggedy-glug of a hot rod at a stop light, and the way it all smooths out into a roar as it accelerates away. Such engines, fitted out with racing cams, will sacrifice performance at low revs to find efficiency at speed. So, it appears we had an accidental hot rod for a moment. An ungoverned and self-generating hot rod. Had it not blown up? My God. We'd still be on our way, I guess, my friends and I, into the silent, airless gulf. Into the dark where two of us, by a different route, have gone already.

It's so strange to come upon a sense of past as a sort of isolated fact out there in the open. What can that mean? Some kind of leak in the system, maybe—too much pressure toward the future finding a weakness at the bend up there where the path turns left by the little tree with the low gray hills and the puffy clouds in the distance. Or as if the here and now were a solution of immiscibles requiring constant stirring—a continuously agitating state of mind, which function breaking down in the glare for whatever reason lets the mixture separate into constituents. Look, the past! (My future heart attack is telling me.) It's right here after all, as you suspected. Quickly now—a napkin sketch before it vanishes.

"The Quality of Ruin at Arcosanti" makes a pretty good title for something. Like a poem by Wallace Stevens. It appears I have a thing for Wallace Stevens. For the idea of him, at least. Whatever that means. It probably only means my sense of what I ought to have received from him but didn't, somehow, quite. Of being left with the convergence toward the meaning of whatever's going on, the marvelous beating of the bush, and then the luminous diversion. (I must watch it here, not glance into his poems while writing this or I'll start picking up his rhythms or his mood, that resignation like a saxophone. What feels like resignation but may only be regret.)

What is the quality of ruin? Western culture has, at times, contrived to render it as spectacle. The vanitas devotion generalized, released into the broad Romantic intuition. We don't have to be religious to believe we're barely here. By the grace of God. As thin as a napkin sketch. Or air. When we were standing in the ruins of the Meteorite Museum, Nancy told me later, what she felt most clearly was the air. The sense of so much air around us and upon us. How remarkable. Just there. The little Meteorite Museum busted open to the sky and, I'm supposing, all the emptiness between the stars beyond it sensed as air. That little bee to mark the center. Hold the emptiness in place for just that moment. Ruins all come crashing down upon our heads because they represent our heads, I think. I think that's what we feel while standing in them—as if, oh my goodness, suddenly our skulls have busted open and we open up, ourselves. Or sense more clearly that clear opening, that inexplicable gulf, that we contain.

I think the quality of ruin is the quality of injury, pathology, sustained, held open, formalized in order to receive us. Come on in and look around at all the air. There's so much air at Arcosanti. Blue sky drifts right through the barrel vaults and gathers in the half domes and the roofless amphitheater. Such thin air I couldn't catch my breath returning up the hill from our excursion in the middle of the afternoon. Ascending back into the pure idea contained in all that "wounded-looking" hand-poured concrete. I come gasping up the hill into this almost theological situation. Pure idea—this pure idea, whatever it is, whatever emerges, intended or not, about our being in the world—expressed as injury.

You know those seventeenth-century vanitas paintings—still lifes, typically Dutch, with all the best things of the world, the gorgeously rendered gold and brass and steel and paper symbols of wealth and human achievement, heaped together with the emblems of mortality: the hourglass, the skull. It's not so much a new idea—such admonitions were depicted in antiquity—as newly resolved in the focus of that technical virtuosity. Our real desires not merely represented here but clarified, refined against the prospect of complete annihilation. Here the brush, like Nancy's pencil, moves "as if it's on the thing itself."

The ripply gleam of copper and the burnish of the gold—my God, it's real. To gaze upon it is to believe it and, thus, have it. Now. The hourglass is stopped. The skull, inert. We know we're as good as dead. In principle. Reducible to ashes, empty landscape. We know that. That's understood. We're barely here. Yet barely here within this captured instant we can have these things so much more beautifully and clearly. That's what's clearly going on beneath the piety. Within our natural injury, our woundedness, there's this exhilaration. You can follow it right down into the simplest terms of childhood. How some little cut from a broken blue glass bottle, say, from reaching into someone's open trash can in the alley in the early 1950s in that clear, precise, and breathless microsecond prior to horror shows your gaudy, precious self to you in a quick ecstatic glimpse. That's what you get in vanitas still lifes. That's what operates to glorify your vegetarian lasagna in the Arcosanti visitors' center café, where such a quality of past and future ruin seems to expand that breathless microsecond out about as far as it can go, seems to expose that precious having of the thing—the gold, the glory, the lasagna, which is to say, of course, the self—to the point that we can hardly stand it. Cannot quite contain ourselves. Such great lasagna in this place. What is this place?

It's probably two in the afternoon. There's no one else except the kitchen staff. We've drifted off the highway into something like the future, which, so curiously, is something like the past. Although we've yet to take the tour and gain a full appreciation of that odd, pervasive archaistic tendency suggested by the classicizing cypresses, haven't formed that sense of ruin that will make this vast interior—with its concrete orbits gaping onto emptiness as empty as that painted on the sides of seventies bubble-windowed vans—seem like the inside of a skull, in spite of this, right off the bat we feel ourselves suspended here in the ambivalence. The airy speculation, the conjecture that's been set up under such a strain, such built-in incompletion that it goes a little vague, a little crumbly at the edges—concrete flaking here and there, the gentle settling of the future into something that receives us yet confuses us exactly like the past. We're like that little girl in the swing in that old photograph, suspended, stilled and specified beyond all doubt. Right here with our lasagna in the moment. And yet blurred somehow, dispersed—as spreading rings disperse the moment of a pebble dropped in water—as a consequence of such a sharp and precious specificity. Oh, Nancy, come on. This is good lasagna. This is good iced tea as well. A futuristic glass of tea. Look at that bulletin board up there. Is that a bulletin board? With bulletins? Those scattered notes and pictures on the wall? Do people understand how precious, here in the future, all that is? How thin the air seems here—around us and upon us. And how clear the facts of ordinary life. How clearly barely here. Right here. Who would have thought? This rudely finished, sandy concrete and these aging blond wood surfaces of simple, vaguely modern—and, hence, vaguely futuristic—chairs and tables seem to recede from us and leave us exposed in the glare of two o'clock in the afternoon—I'm going to say exactly two in the afternoon, *a las dos de la tarde*—to the very point of the endless, precious moment cleanly, blankly as a photograph or the bull ring. Gorgeous, bloody-red lasagna. This is my body. Here we are. Oh, come on, Nancy. This is my blood.

PART TWO

1

I'VE BUILT A LITTLE OBSERVATORY ON THE DECK IN MY BACKYARD.
It's not a proper observatory, insofar as it does not provide an
isolated concrete pier for the instrument. So, whenever my dog
Rocky, in his doghouse there on the deck, decides to scratch his
butt, the image goes to hell. Vibrations multiplied by a factor of
four or five hundred through the eyepiece, you just take a break
and wait for things to settle down. It's frustrating and yet kind of
sweet in a way, to sense these intimate concerns projected out
into the heavens. Which may serve to represent a point of principle here, I think.

It is, moreover, a lousy place for an observatory. Under all
these trees. A very limited patch of sky straight overhead and to
the north. And just enough of a slot to the south to give me half
an hour or so of Mars in its course so low in its current, other-

wise favorable opposition. If I'm out there by one-thirty in the morning, shutter open, scope turned on, I'll catch it coming through the leaves. Then Rocky stirring. As if everything were shivering, straining with me to receive some hint of surface features, polar regions, something like our world up there, displaced. Removed from us. It feels a little like averted vision, somehow. In a broader sense. That trick, if you remember, whereby objects in the telescopic field too faint to be observed directly may be glimpsed out of the corner of your eye. You look away and there it is—the star, the shaky, leafy ordinary world. Up there. Removed and reacquired. I have a little folding drawing table set up in the dome next to the telescope, where I attempt to go directly at the indirection, as it were, with brush and ink, straight through the eyepiece. Paint the strain, the longing even, by the loosest possible means—to get these brushy, smeary, un-Lowellian renderings of the planet. One per night. Try not to lie. Yet try to fix it in the inky-black surrounding. Let the edges of the disk seem to emerge. Do not assume it's really there. Or not so clearly, matter-of-factly as those templates with preprinted disks that amateurs would use back in the days when drawing still could capture subtleties the simpleminded cameras of the era overlooked. That low in the sky, you're looking through a lot of fluctuating atmosphere. You bring to it a squint—as through a crack in the fence at something. What is that? As if you weren't quite sure. Be quiet, Rocky. What did Nancy say? As if the pencil or the brush were "on the thing itself." To bring it "into you." Well, I can't manage that. So try to paint the squinting. Paint the blur. The in-between, I guess, in a way. She says that opening of the dome, the shutter—that slit in the smooth white hemisphere—reminds her of a hatching egg's first crack with something peeping out. I wish I'd thought of that. It's raining now. And probably will be for another day or two. I'll have to wait. But it's a good tight little dome that's shown no tendency to leak. The hemisphere—cast polyethylene from a company that also produces shelters for farm animals; God, I love it—is translucent. It's like milk glass. So you go inside in the day, in the rain to check—you never know—and there's this uniform gray light in there. This cool gray light and the sound of rain and these smudgy pale gray renderings on the watercolor paper sort of blurring into the sound, as it seems. The whole idea sort of fading at the edges as a stroke of ink will do into wet paper.

You can buy an astronomical camera now with CCD technology and complex image processing built right in to punch through atmospheric blur and render images just about as clear as those achieved from space. They make you gasp—less at the level of detail, I think, than at the sense of groundlessness. The feeling that you're floating out there somewhere. Having lost the blur, you've also lost your reference. Lost that sense of place (from which to sense displacement) in exchange for a detailed report from a smaller, separate, specialized intelligence that doesn't care or wonder where it is in all of this. That has no need to look away because it has no place in the first place. As it were.

My first real telescope—so marvelously distinct from the dime-store spyglass or my minimally functional plastic reproduction of the famous Hale two-hundred-inch at Palomar, or even that monstrous six-foot-long refractor with the cardboard tube my father bought for me (from an ad, I think, in one of those popular science magazines), and which, secured by means of a flimsy bracket atop a stepladder, had to be craned about the heavens with the same difficulty as would have attended the operation of its ungainly seventeenth-century antecedents to produce the most discouraging, though perhaps historically faithful, views of blobby stars and featureless glare of moon like water pouring down a pipe—but that first real one, with its 2.4-inch achromatic objective lens in a white-enameled aluminum tube on a shiny black cast-aluminum mount with a sturdy wooden tripod, had intention, had adjustments, had this wonderful complication toward so simple, pure, and rarefied a purpose. More important, though, it had a fitted box of a kind of plywood made from Philippine mahogany whose earthy cedary fragrance seemed to involve the very concept of it all, seemed to emerge from that whole astronomical business and eventually to sustain and even characterize those longings I attached—much as the censer's fumes may seem to attach and sustain the faith—to the instrument itself delivered unto me that Christmas by my mom and dad and the Unitron Instrument Company. For years—well into adulthood—I could summon the actual fragrance, bring it forth by act of will, the aromatic fact to activate those primitive parts of the brain, which is to say of course the heart, wherein the smell of the earth was felt to carry up, and carry one along, into the higher regions. What a curious and exhilarating intimacy in that. That sense of approach. Of immanence. The earthy scent imparted to the heavens. Such a nearness to the vastness. Not unlike, perhaps, what John Dee must have felt to receive into that little stone the celestial messenger.

I've lost it now. I've thought too much about it and I've lost it. The ability—it seems to have been an ability—to open myself up to it now and then for whatever reason, long past childhood, suddenly pause in the midst of ordinary life and let it drift back in, the delicate earthy smell of outer space, the meaning of it. Overwhelming sense of meaning as a pure emotional, prearticulate fact or personal state, perhaps, accompanied by a drawing in of breath in preparation for, who knows, the understanding that should follow as the lightning bolt the path of ionization through the sky. I try to recover it indirectly—still expecting understanding, I suppose. But the closest I can get, I think, may be remembering the scent of my first girlfriend on a shirt I kept, for a year or more, unlaundered in my closet. I was seventeen. We'd parted for some reason. But I kept the shirt, which kept, for a while, the thought. Although of course it's not the same—one's longing has an object here. It seems complete, if unfulfilled. You hold the shirt to your face and feel yourself extended toward that thing, exquisite terminus—extended and, in a sense, received. That's that, you sigh. It's done. The old transaction reenacted. Charge released, the matter settled for a while until the question should arise again, accumulating gradually toward that moment in the closet and that discharge, fainter and fainter every time.

It's not the same. And yet, and yet. You bring the fragrance to your face and close your eyes. You look away for it—that's what it means to close your eyes. I think. You make that leap, draw in your breath, to find yourself out there, to mean yourself away from yourself like that. One doesn't know what one is doing at that age, of course. One stumbles into the gap to find the intimacies required to leave a fragrance on one's shirt. You close your eyes into the gap. You look away and there it is. And there you are.

I usually try to get a glimpse while it's still coming through the branches and the leaves. If there's a breeze, the image flickers in and out and I can gain a sense of where to place the first pale watery marks. There's not much time. Nor, as it seems, much hope for this. I have no gift for it. The brush upon the paper seems so sad, so disinclined to find a gesture. On the other hand, what gesture can there be? As for a spray of bamboo, say? A drape of waterfall? The ancient sweep of Fuji with its slapdash skirt of pines? I console myself to think that you cannot find a gesture from within the world to represent the world. These squinty observations, then, I want to think a kind of redirected gaze. Averted vision. Looking away for it. A way to slip the ordinary world into the corner of your eye—to reacquire it. So of course I stumble into it. Accumulating clumsy dabs—a roll of paper towels at hand to smear it out and let me try again—toward some agreement as it drifts across the gap into the catalpa tree, whose huge and overlapping heart-shaped leaves will close the show.

It won't stop raining. Mars is past its opposition. What have these remarks to do with one another? Like two statements for translation on a foreign language test. Yet to me the meanings tug and strain each other. And I think there's something here inside the dome, in the rain to check for leaks, in the cool gray light, like standing in the closet with the shirt pressed to my face. A bit like that. Good Lord. It all comes down to that. How could it not? One of those trivial profundities: All longing is the same. When I was six or so—before I'd turned so much as a dime-store spyglass toward the heavens—I conceived to build a telescope. Or something like "conceived." It's hard to say. But as there must be more than unexamined impulse in those Epipaleolithic cave wall paintings, so, perhaps with this. A sort of invocation of the principle, I guess. Though I remember my regret at the inadequacy. Despair, in fact. The nailing of four old green-painted planks, from a broken garden swing or something, into a long square tube to mount upon a wheelbarrow, getting down to look up through it at the air above the garage. A lens, of course, was out of the question. I decided, therefore, it would have to be enough to imagine, merely imagine, to propose to myself, that one might manage to rig some sort of vessel that could pour a sheet of water—drape of waterfall—across the open end where the objective lens should be, and that, as water is known to distort the shapes of objects seen within it, so might bodies far beyond be magnified by that same property, albeit so erratically and fleetingly as to require great patience on the part of the observer. Limitations with regard to elevating such an instrument above the horizontal didn't seem to be a concern. It was enough. I'd done what I could do. And that was pretty sad. I knew. Heartbreaking in a way—to the extent heartbreak was possible back then. And I suppose it was, if fleeting and erratic. I remember looking at it in the rain out there in the backyard, thinking what a clumsy, desperate proposition—what an undistinguished thing out there like that, as wet and sad as any ordinary backyard thing, old garden swing or pile of boards or whatever in the rain. How can desire get jammed into a thing like that? Into what realm and toward what object should it seek to project itself by such a poor, unlikely instrument?

In 1926, Albert Ingalls, associate editor at the *Scientific American* magazine, and Russell Porter, Arctic explorer, artist, and engineer, whose subtle and luminous cutaway visualizations of the two-hundred-inch Hale Telescope shall remain, I suspect, the ultimate expression of the mechanical draftsman's art, collaborated to produce a slender manual titled *Amateur Telescope Making,* which, expanding in its subsequent editions to incorporate the record of response toward what now seems to have been a golden age between the wars, before TV, of interest and invention in the field, became, by the time my friend Vernon Grissom brought one along to one of our semi-regular dinners at the "Little El Fenix" Mexican buffet on Lovers Lane in Dallas, Texas, in the fifties, an intimidating, dark maroon-bound volume of an almost biblical density and heft. Among the indecipherable diagrams and formulae and renderings of mirror-testing patterns, the impossible machinery of it all (my sad, unpenetrating gaze reflecting back to me, above my enchiladas, from the semi-glossy pages), there were photographs of amateurs with telescopes they'd made. These I could contemplate, at least. These somewhat grainy 1920s–1930s moments, posed and self-sufficient, with the thing itself presented. On my desk, I've got a reprint of the 1945 edition, probably the same.

⋆

HERE IS "A SIX-INCH REFLECTOR WITH DOUBLE-YOKE MOUNTING, MADE by Winston Juengst of Tillson, N.Y." Young Winston stands by an ivied wall, it looks like, hands in knickers pockets, sweater, possibly a tie beneath, hair neatly combed and parted high off-center like the golfer Bobby Jones's and gazing down into the front end of his instrument with studious detachment. He has done it. Made this telescope himself. Although the double-yoke arrangement, built of wooden planks, appears rickety and difficult to use. It seems enough for now to stand there in what looks like afternoon in the grainy, dusty 1920s with his hair combed, with his telescope, beside the ivied wall.

★

"A PORTABLE 12-INCH REFLECTOR MADE BY H. L. ROGERS OF Toronto" is displayed with a child of ten or so in heavy coat and cap and gloves beside it in the snow. The massive instrument (which classifies as "portable" by virtue, I suppose, of the towable dolly that supports it) tilts toward vertical on its counterweighted equatorial mount. It towers above the child, who stands quite stiff and straight in the cold to lend a clear, obedient sense of scale. ("Look right at me. Hands down to your side. Smile.") To the left, the edge of the house or a garage. Behind, a fence, a leafless tree.

★

"A SQUARE BOX TUBE FOR A SIX-INCH MIRROR. TELESCOPE MADE BY Hugh G. Boutell of the Bureau of Standards." He's in a three-piece suit, stiff 1920s collar, watch chain, spectacles, fedora, small mustache. He stands with his well-constructed instrument at the bottom of the steps to his front door, one hand to the rear of the angled tube—a light, proprietary touch to show that he's not just there for scale. That he's responsible—against all expectations, maybe; such a slight, constrained, meticulous-looking Bureau of Standards sort of guy to have produced a thing like this and get his picture in the book, along with all the other similar accomplishments unreferenced by the stern, instructional text in which they float like family pictures tucked into the family Bible. These old photographs recede—invite, require a deeper sort of concentration. The essential, insubstantial present moment seems more precious the more distant as such photographs, old photographs, are felt to have detached from us—receded beyond our sense of them, of the ones we're always taking all the time, as a sort of spillage from the ordinary moment we inhabit. At some point they seem released, adrift out there, the present moment even thinner, less substantial than we thought, our thoughts about it more compressed upon the slightly grainy, semi-glossy patinating surface. Just as with that little girl in the swing in 1910 or so, we cannot help but feel concern and bring a strained yet tender scrutiny to bear upon the fading human fact of it, the emotional circumstances. He did what? He built a telescope? It seems so odd. A tidy gentleman like that. What does he want to see? Is something wrong, do you think? What *did* the neighbors think? If they thought much of anything. They might have seen him posing for the picture. Probably taken by his wife—we can imagine in an apron holding one of those foldout cameras with the bellows. "There, like that. Don't move." What is this thing? And what is his intention? At the bottom of the tube—of screwed-together wooden boards—there is a mirror. Where he rests his hand. The light—what light there is at night, so strange: the moon, the stars, who knows—comes in at the other end, which is angled up, the open end where, just inside, another mirror, very tiny, held by wires or metal strips at forty-five degrees, directs the focused beam from the primary mirror into the eyepiece at the side. It all seems so obscure, so indirect, so secret. Like a peep show. It would look a bit like that, of course—a sort of box with a sort of hole that you're supposed to squint through at some sort of naughty goings-on. You imagine him like that as well, fedora in his hand and leaning over, eye pressed to it—that same awkwardness, uncertainty. That terrible and timid curiosity. And surely, don't you think, a similar longing.

★

I HAVE HAD FOR MANY YEARS A PARTICULAR IMAGE—NEVER FAR BElow the surface of my thoughts—from *Amateur Telescope Making*. One of the Russell Porter drawings found throughout and usually to illustrate some point of fabrication or design but in this case—as I remembered it from Vernon Grissom's copy, I suppose, not having had one of my own until quite recently—detached, more ornamental and expressive of the enterprise in general. Over time I'd reimagined and enlarged it as one will. I'd made it into a sort of frontispiece or something. So, at first I was bewildered not to find it in my reprint of the 1945 edition. Then surprised to spot it as a filler, a vignette about the size of a pair of postage stamps, an afterthought to keep the eye from losing its way in the emptiness below a half-page table of solar-to-sidereal time conversion figures. Something was needed there and I suppose they had this drawing. I extend my creaky desktop magnifier lamp. And there it is. Essentially as remembered—though I'd filtered out the Norman Rockwellish condescension of it. But that's it. It's good. It's still okay. I sigh as I drift below the tabulations into this. I really do. A little sigh. A little window

onto a full moon rising just above an old board fence and glow-
ing through the gaps into a small backyard where a lanky figure
squats upon what seems to be an upturned bushel basket at the
eyepiece of a long refractor trained above the fence upon the
rising moon and balanced insecurely atop a stepladder. I'd forgotten that as well. The stepladder. Goodness. Norman Rock-
well notwithstanding, there is something in it. Look at how the
moonlight pours across and through the fence into the yard—a
1920s sort of backyard, earlier maybe. Porter was born in 1871,
so where's he going to go with this? It's *Our Town*. All the emblems of a classic domesticity are present in the moonlight:
clothesline, rain barrel, cellar door, cat on the fence. Three hundred years to get it down to these essentials. Settled in upon
these shores. And from an open gable window, his wife leans
into the moonlight. Gazing down. Too small, the halftone screen
too coarse, for us to make out her expression. Just as well. We
can imagine her withdrawing to the bed to watch the slowly
changing angle of the moonlight on the wall and feel the night
air start to cool. And sense the emptiness next to her as a sort of
premonition—not to recognize as such but just to feel—and
pull the covers up a little. That her lanky, somewhat comically
configured husband, right outside, should feel so far away.

★

THE RAIN HAS STOPPED, THE SKY IS CLEAR, THE FIREFLIES OUT, OLD
Rocky, lame and in decline these many years, has breathed his
last, so it's just me and I'm back at it. Mars appears between the
trees at kinder hours. Every night a little earlier. If the image
isn't steady it's my fault—my shifting, breathing. My uneasiness.

My animal discomfort. Good old Rocky. Mighty barker. Killer of possums. Shaker of worlds.

I keep expecting to acquire a measure of competence at this. I've lightly penciled three-inch circles—nine in ranks of three to make a square array on the thirty-by-twenty-two-inch water-color paper—brushing the background black around each as I come to it, the edge allowed to bleed or smear or dry-brush into the disk a bit, the features, as I'm able to discern them now and then in furtive glimpses through the leaves, the turbulent atmo-sphere, in quick, diluted brushings with the same brush dipped in water, back and forth between the eyepiece and the paper. Dip and wipe with paper towel and try again and hope to catch a moment's clarity, then hold it long enough to make a mark and hope the marks accumulate somehow convincingly. What con-stitutes convincingly? Well, that's a problem, isn't it?

Brush and ink is not the way to render Mars. It's how to render—if you're competent—the things of the world reduced to gesture. To the act of pointing at them, in a way—or at the place where they should be. More a summoning than a copy-ing. Behold these dry persimmons, this bamboo, this splash of bird upon the merest, thinnest brushstroke of a branch as if such things, the things we know, pop into being out of nothing but an act of will, resolve themselves into, become, themselves, the act of seeing. Which is to say the act of being in the world—which Mars, the telescopic fact, seems quite beyond. There is no deep, habitual sense of Mars to summon with such ease it feels implicit in the brush. It's hard to imagine someone saying of a painting of the planet, Ah, yes: That's it. You've got it per-fectly. A couple of strokes reveal the very essence. There's no essence. Only surface. To be rendered, properly rendered, with a pencil and a kind of scientific trepidation. With that delicate, fearful longing adolescent girls bring to their first attempts to draw a pony. Lines and smudges shift about. Is it a pony yet? A world? I swear, all longing is the same. Look at the rigorous series of drawings E. E. Barnard produced of Mars in the 1890s through the great thirty-six-inch refractor at Lick Observatory. Though it's usual to present such images masked with background solid black, his notebooks show them drawn, with scribbled notes, on numbered blue-ruled pages. Just like what we scribbled on in school, our concentration lost to ponies, rocket ships, whatever beckoned. It was what we had before us. Notebook paper—horizontal lines, imposed to guide our horizontal thoughts, constraining here, a little sadly, all our longings to the surface like a trellis. As if longings might belong to some assignment. Now we're going to draw the things we'd love to attain but never can. Well, that would tend to kill it, wouldn't it? Wouldn't you think? The imposition of a sense of matter-of-factness to such things. I hated blue-ruled notebook paper. Even though I scribble on it still—a blue-ruled legal pad. It represents the flatness, the prescription of our measured understanding. The extension, the attenuation of it—on and on, it felt like way back there in grade school. You could see it never ended. Those blue lines continued on and on, one notebook to the next, year after year. Sometimes you'd write "The End" to something, but it never was. It never is. The flatness keeps on going. Straight on out—as I used to dream in dreams of Buffalo, New York—"from under the dark and snowy trees right into space." We never lose it, never leave it, I'm convinced.

Though now I seem to be resigned. To the assignment, I suppose.

I've come to feel, in fact, that there's something sweet about it. The prescriptive, dry procedure of our longing. Something sweet about Barnard's meticulous renderings on blue-ruled notebook paper, image flattened as if held against the paper by the lines, by habit of thought, like some botanical specimen pressed in place to represent the broader fact. The fact of place in this case, as it seems. Of place in general. The world. It seems so strange to find it way out there. But, sure enough, you look away, avert your eyes, and there it is. His delicate, penciled scribble-scrabble flat as it can be within his perfect, compassed circle. There's no darkening or curving of the lines out toward the edge to indicate the mass, the roundness of the thing. There is no thing. There's only surface. Flat and random as the accidental planetary surface in that photo of the crater wall I took at Meteor Crater through that clunky public telescope. And yet how sweet, how clear, resigned to render it so carefully and dutifully. How touching, even, given Barnard's lack of formal education (William Sheehan's biography documents his miserable youth in Nashville during the Civil War and after), as if here to find a schoolboy's simple tongue-protruding diligence—at last, held in reserve till now—directed up as openly and earnestly as later, by some other schoolchild, down upon that little painted neighborhood of plastic Monopoly houses Nancy bought in Corsicana for a dollar.

"In 1956 when I was eleven years old, there occurred an unusually favorable opposition of Mars," begins the second page of a sort of observational notebook of my own that I've been at for the last ten years, and which I find has fallen into parallel with what I'm writing here, or maybe vice versa. It's all brush and ink on very large sheets of watercolor paper, and the reason for that setup with the little drawing table in the observatory dome. But anyway, the somewhat loose and scattered narrative that forms around occasional attempts to paint the planet through the eyepiece starts with this. I love what seems the portent of it, I must say. "In 1956 when I was eleven . . ." As if to suggest that from this event we shall be led to understand some strange and powerful consequence.

Back then we still had books in school that showed canals on Mars. The movies *Red Planet Mars, Invaders from Mars,* and *The War of the Worlds* had all come out not long before and begun to trickle down into the Saturday morning kid shows at the neighborhood movie theaters, into the popular apprehension. With Korea and McCarthy fading out, I think there must have been a clearing for a thing like this. Above the low-roofed postwar houses, lawns of yellow, dusty, dry Bermuda grass. Late-summer evenings bringing people out to gaze up at the apparition, brighter and brighter every night. It hadn't been like that before. It was conspicuous now, and sort of red, in fact. Most people—people not inclined to pay attention to the sky—knew what it was, that it approached somehow, whatever that might mean.

My mom read somewhere that a local astronomy club (the one that I would later join as a junior member) had invited the public out to their property south of town to witness the event through members' telescopes on the night of opposition. Mars would be well-placed in the sky and its diameter would be

24.8 arc seconds—just about as big as it can get at thirty-five million miles. Just miles. Not astronomical units or light-years—most of us had heard of light-years. Only miles. You could imagine miles. A thousand miles was a long way but imaginable. I remember once on a trip to Colorado with my parents and some family friends, we crested some great rise to see the dead-straight two-lane highway dip away into a distance (who knows—maybe that same distance that impressed me decades later coming back the other way), but such a distance that you caught your breath to see the highway narrow to a thread and disappear into the hazy line of foothills. One of the grown-ups in the front seat—either my father or the father of my two back-seat companions (he was a scientist and liked to think up intellectual contests for the kids)—made note of the mileage at that point, requiring each of us to estimate the miles across the valley. What the brother and sister guessed I can't recall—but something reasonable, I'm sure. One thousand miles, I ventured. I think it turned out to be about twenty. But one thousand miles, I said. No hesitation. Look at that. You think of a thousand miles, then think of what a thousand miles should look like, and that's it. And it still is to me. At any rate, a thousand miles seems ponderable, imaginable. Just string a bunch of those together, pretty soon you're there. A bunch of long straight roads that take your breath away into the vacuum and you're there.

And so, on that evening of the closest approach, my mom and I set out to find this place, to get a telescopic glimpse. This was before the major freeways, so it took a while to get through town, past neighborhoods decreasingly familiar into regions tending rural, scattered houses here and there, sometimes with people in the front yards, in the fading light and, I imagined, waiting for the planet to appear above the fields. It seemed to me that we ourselves approached. As civilization thinned and darkness gathered we were on our way to a conjunction—of ideas, I'd like to say, as if I'd any of my own at that age, which of course I didn't—of impressions, then. Impressions of the ordinary world and some unthinkable alternative.

At some point not too far from the Dallas/Ellis County line—quite dark by now, just open fields with barbed-wire fences, now and then a pale green mercury-vapor lamp on a telephone pole—we made a turn at a lonely service station where they had a telescope set up, a pretty serious-looking one, with a sign that offered peeks at Mars for fifty cents or maybe a dollar. We were getting close to something more than a viewing opportunity, though. It seemed to me. It seemed to me, in the dark and the general unfamiliarity, that the strangeness of another world impinged, pressed in upon us, might be sensed in its immensity, if not exactly glimpsed, out there somewhere above the trees. A lot of trees now, on both sides of a gravel road that dipped and rose. And other headlights up ahead. Some handmade signs. A haze of dust. We slowed to a gentle crunch of gravel, windows down. Cars lined the road on either side—no place to park. And people everywhere, emerging from their cars or climbing the little hill with flashlights playing back and forth in the grass. So many flashlights, as if evidence of Mars might be discovered on the ground. So many people, as if all had been just waiting for the call to gather way out here in the dark in the middle of nowhere. We couldn't even see the telescopes. Just flashlights moving up the hill—as if toward some disaster or some miracle. Like candles, I imagine now, toward something for whose apprehension telescopes were really not required. We turned around and went back home. A pretty long drive out there and back for very little to report. Yet I cannot recall a sense of disappointment.

★

ON THE COVER OF SHEEHAN'S BIOGRAPHY IS A PHOTOGRAPH OF Barnard with the thirty-six-inch refractor—in diameter half again larger than Lowell's, and altogether dwarfing it in terms of mass and bulk. How does one pose with such a thing? As with the Sphinx or the Taj Mahal, it's hard to know just how to situate oneself. In a slightly rumpled three-piece suit, detached from his usual focused, purposeful position at the eyepiece, he appears a bit uncertain how to find the proper attitude; where best, there at the working end of things, among the jumble of controls and instrumentation—all the adjusting wheels and knobs and smaller ancillary telescopes—to place his elbow, how to bring his folded hand to rest his head against it in a natural-looking way. Is there a natural-looking way? He seems to intend a sort of ease that isn't easy. Or, at least, not here. But here (at the working end of things) is where he needs to be, as if just stepped away from the eyepiece to reveal himself—discoverer, quite recently to great acclaim, of Jupiter's fifth moon—as a regular person just like you or me. We feel invited, even (surely there's an eyepiece there somewhere within that tangle of instruments). He stands as if beside some monstrous carnival attraction, waiting for someone to step right up and take the chance, to satisfy that terrible and timid curiosity. To risk, from such an instrument, such stillness, such exhilarating emptiness you wouldn't think to hold a child up to it. Come on, honey, have a look. Not on your life. She'd wriggle free and run away.

★

ABOVE MY DESK, ABOVE MY CANTILEVERED MAGNIFYING DESK LAMP, which I sometimes move about to simulate the creaky passage of the sun across the sky, there hangs a drawing by my dear dead friend, the artist Doug MacWithey, that depicts the sutural surfaces of a pair of ancient human cranial fragments known as the Swanscombe skull. Recovered from stratified gravels near the Thames at the town of Swanscombe in Kent in 1935 and '36 (a third discovery would be made in '55), the "skull" consisted, at the time of the 1938 report—a copy of which I'd loaned to Doug—of an occipital and a single parietal bone from a context datable to the "middle Acheulean," which is to say to around four hundred thousand years ago. The bones, displaying very little wear, had separated from each other, and from the missing cranial plates, along the sutures—so these corrugated seams were well preserved and deemed sufficiently of interest as to merit special attention in the report, which reproduced, in full-sized photographs, all five irregular cross sections, one thick pitted and furrowed arc above the other like a display of crude parentheses assemblable to set apart some primitive idea. Or, as Doug felt, a sort of kit—a set of ill-made drafting curves—toward the design and manufacture of the self, a still-experimental consciousness. He loved the alchemical/theological sense of that. That something pure and clear might be accessible to rough, imperfect means. That truth, in one form or another, might be whacked and bent and struggled into shape. Which, in his sculpture, seemed to constitute a basic working principle: that truth was best approached with brutal instruments, attacked, to the disdain of anything that looked like craftsmanship (and, therefore, resolution) in his bashed-together wood and sheet steel pieces hung by cables from the ceiling, sometimes placed upon the floor.

His pencil drawings, on the other hand, could not have been more painfully constrained. He'd tend to fasten on some image out of ancient mystical or natural historical authority and capture it, lay over it this netlike penciled grid to make it easier to copy and enlarge. Some shrub or tree or portion thereof from some obscure medieval herbal, say, would take him weeks to render, square by square, in that dense, excruciating process. Less like drawing than tattooing into the paper till the image, from a distance, looked dead black as if bled into itself, a stain of itself which, on close examination, would reveal itself as teeming with submerged detail—schematic little shapes suggesting leaves or fruit or swarms of paramecia—subordinate facts like ornament.

So this is how he'd tend to work back then—in the nineties when we'd meet at a Mexican restaurant near his house for lunch on Fridays, float ideas, ideas about ideas, above our enchiladas. What's the deal with enchiladas? Do our thoughts just naturally elevate above such simple, earthy gratifications? Anyway, it's how he'd work. He'd either go straight at it, grapple with it out there in the open, as it were, attempt to fabricate a physical idea, or he'd go receptive, and simply capture, as a specimen for study (pressed beneath that unerased rectangular grid like notebook paper), some idea long out of use and, so, released in a sense to represent the species—the idea of the idea—to be subjected to analysis. Here's what our understanding looks like captured, pressed, and stained—the way biologists treat specimens to bring out certain features. "Drawn to death," he liked to say. And over here—hung from the rafters (curatorial nightmare) and threatening to come apart where nails too large have split the ends of the one-by-twos that hold the thing together, nails that seem to have been driven with a rock—here's what it looks like as it happens, as you think it, as it rises from the flat extended surface of the mind and tries to fold into the air.

What's going on, then, with his drawing of the Swanscombe skull cross sections? He seems to sample, here, that scientific sampling that he imitates. Examining, in effect, his own constrained, receptive method as applied here to that struggle at the level of the still-experimental self itself—this set of brutal drafting instruments toward something like an idea, like a consciousness four hundred thousand years ago.

Such enchilada talk can seem too rarefied. Can seem to drift away into the mariachi music, out the door into the fragrant afternoon. But there's a sadness in the science here—no less than in those tragic, violent ballads called *corridos*. Look at how built in the injury is. How readily and naturally we fall apart. The ruin—which is what this is about, I think; the quality of ruin—is implicit. So, how natural to take this clear and mournfully objective fact and make it a memento—like pressed flowers, like a funerary photograph, hand-tinted (drawn to death) to appeal to a deeper intuition: How the air, the vacuum, moves within the parts of us. How we cannot contain ourselves. How this experimental broken self (of modern cranial capacity four hundred thousand years ago) suggests as well—though science is less certain on this point—the broken heart.

To the right of my desk, on a high bookshelf, in a little easel frame, I have a photograph of Doug at eight or nine years old, I'd guess, on Christmas morning, given to me by his widow, Karan Verma. Oh my goodness. Precious child. So beaten up throughout his childhood in that large and largely self-destructive family—so diminished and endangered and ignored. Somehow someone has come upon him by himself, produced this photographic fact of him. (Those ornaments behind, against the darkness of the Christmas tree—my God, how like symbolic fruit, schematic paramecia.) He's sitting on the floor among his presents and he smiles up at the camera, knows to do that. (He was always good with people—good at openings though he hated them.) He has a model airplane and one of those nasty stuffed baby alligators—grinning, glass-eyed, up at him as he leans over a little drawing board, a lap desk sort of thing with "Douglas" printed across the top and a pad of paper he holds flat with his right hand, pencil in the other. Look as if you're drawing something, he's been told. I'm guessing this is quite exceptional—a personalized gift like this. And worth recording. See—it's not so bad. He smiles. No visible wounds. The little glass-eyed alligator smiling too. It's not so bad exactly now. Within the flash. Within this sixtieth of a second all is possible, shall always have been possible: the Christmas tree behind him, the little drawing desk and, look there by his foot, the brutal instruments themselves, the basic tools. They look like used ones. From the bottom of the tool box. Little hammer. Saw. A screwdriver. Single plastic-handled screwdriver. That's so sad. Hey, we could throw these in, I guess. And yet it's all he'll ever need. Is this the Acheulean moment? The beginning? Look as if you're drawing something. Making something. Look as if you haven't had your own skull broken. Haven't been tossed through a plate-glass window twice by your big brother. Busted up so many times, so many ways. Of course it had to figure into everything—that microsecond of ecstatic fascination children seem to have with injury, that terrible revelation, but extended, in his case, throughout his life. Into his art. His love for empty ruined houses, for example, whose interiors he'd photograph. The vanitas-like images of skulls in earlier pieces. How the bashing of a thing together seems so close to bashing it apart.

When Doug and Karan lived in Galveston, she told me, there occurred one summer a very powerful storm that flooded all the streets and brought out all the toads. The toads were everywhere, especially in the streets. And as the water receded and the traffic resumed, toads perished in great numbers. So that after the streets had dried and the summer sun had been out a while there were these desiccated, flattened toads all over the place. Which circumstance produced in Doug a strange and wild excitement that impelled him, at one point on their evening stroll as they encountered a particularly impressive concentration, to race home to fetch a suitable container, telling Karan to stay and keep an eye on things. She's pretty sure that's what he said. Which she interpreted to mean the toads. That she should stay and keep an eye on the toads. To make it clear to passersby, potential gatherers presumably, that these were spoken for. How long she waited I have no idea. But long enough to contemplate the course her life had taken, I suspect. Doug trotted back with a plastic bag, collected maybe twenty specimens, eventually transferring them to a shirt box, where he kept them, rattly shadows, until he himself was flattened by a heart attack years later, never having found a use for them. Unwilling to discard them.

When they moved from the coast to the little Texas town of Corsicana to escape the damp and the hurricanes and the inexplicable (given how he loved the island) sogginess of spirit that oppressed him there and practically extinguished his creative will, the shirt box with its contents came along. He kept it under one of his several drawing tables on the second floor of the airy, many-windowed nineteenth-century former Odd Fellows hall they purchased. Karan says he'd take it out from time to time and gaze into it with this curious attitude of consultation as if pondering the tarot or the oracle bones or something. Something having to do with fate and death and meaning. Love and terror. The compression of experience. The way you think you're just about to get somewhere, then *whap*. Your brother throws you through a window. Huns arrive upon the scene. The Inquisition takes an interest. Volcanism. Periodic glaciation. All the hardships of the Pleistocene. The ebb and flow of paradise across our slow migration to induce a faint suspicion of our mortal selves. That clear, abiding injury that opens us, admits into the cranial vault a glimmer like the flickering of traffic into a darkened room at night.

★

TO OPEN THE DOME OF MY LITTLE OBSERVATORY I HAVE TO CLIMB A stepladder placed outside to reach the bottom of the up-and-over shutter, which requires a mighty shove to start the process. When it jams, as it usually does, I have to climb back down to retrieve from just inside the door a three-foot wooden pole with a rubber tip, whereby, atop the ladder again, to impart an even mightier shove to open it all the way—or as far as it wants to go. It is an awkward, even violent, operation. Like you're busting something open. And, as Nancy has observed, there is about it something of the cracking egg. The Humpty Dumpty broken skull. *Whap,* goes the shutter when you shove it with sufficient force to make it slide across the nylon rails to strike the stop. And all that complex instrumentation, all that lovely, delicate optical and mechanical stuff within exposed to the air. To so much air, as Nancy said about the ruins. And inside with night descending, sounds of insects, sounds of traffic, stars like flickerings of traffic, cool air falling through the slit, it does feel faintly like a scrape or a cut exposed to air. To all that air and emptiness as, standing in the alley behind my house at five years old cut by a piece of glass the concentrated color of the sky, I felt exposed.

Observatories—big ones—tend to perch dramatically on prominences like ruins. They seem naturally to accede to that Romantic eighteeth/nineteenth-century station. To extend that mood of lofty introspection. You think to lift thine eyes? Well, step right up and have a look through this. They have that quality of ruin, after all—of ruin formalized. That thrill of vast exposure as those great bi-parting shutters (of the classic domes like that atop Mount Palomar) break open, split the vault, admit into our dark interior a flickering, exhilarating emptiness traversable (as I suspect we cannot help but feel) by endless long flat roads. Do you remember *Alphaville*? That curious, arty science-fiction film by Jean-Luc Godard? How at the end the intergalactic secret agent flees back home across the emptiness of space to his home galaxy. That's how the overvoice describes it—"interstellar space." But we can see he's only driving down the highway at night, the streetlamps flashing by like stars, reflected in the windshield of the car he has stolen. Why should that seem so remarkable, I wondered when I first saw it. Why should that take your breath away? Then make you sigh. Become a thing to contemplate for fifty years? I suppose I might have started this whole thing with that—as Frazer's *Golden Bough* begins with one of those misty, mythological paintings by Turner, which evokes the scene of a terrible ancient ritual so compelling and mysterious it requires a twelve-volume study to explain it. Were I less diffuse, more organized, I might have tried to develop this whole project from that final scene in *Alphaville*. A little thing like that. Like Frazer tugging at the dangling thread then noting, for twelve volumes, what unravels. Out from under us in this case, I suspect, the whole flat fabric of experience—so level is our gaze no matter what; so deeply, hopefully, and sweetly migratory, always longing for arrival, for the stillness, I've decided, of that tiny bee that hovers in the window of the ruins of the Meteorite Museum at the center of the world.

What takes your breath away, I think, is how direct it seems—how clear, unmetaphorical, immediately acceptable a way to think about it. No big deal. Just tilt your head a bit and there it is. As it has always been—your level gaze tilts up; the vertical is just a special case of horizontal. Surely some bizarre geometry exists to formalize it—interstellar space describable as highway. Stars as streetlamps flashing by. Of course, of course. We've always known.

★

NOW HERE'S "AN EIGHT-INCH REFLECTOR MADE BY JOSEPH KUHN, WIS-consin Rapids, Wisc." The telescope is mounted on a pedestal that's sunk into a buried concrete base in his backyard. The grass around it scuffed away like that around a drinking fountain in some schoolyard. He's a man of considerable girth, his hands in his pockets, holding back his open suit coat to present his ample paunch to the rear of his instrument, impinging on it somewhat. Somewhat oddly. Why does he want to have his picture taken standing there like that? You'd think his wife (as we imagine) would have encouraged him to find a better pose (How does one pose with such a thing?), to come around and act like he is looking through it. Button his coat and keep his hands out of his pockets. Bring his eye up to the eyepiece in a natural-looking way. But he just stands there looking down as if he's lost in concentration on some point of craftsmanship that needs correcting. Something not quite as it should be, he remembers, there at the bottom end of things where, in its cell, resides the mirror, in the process of whose complicated, graduated grinding and then polishing so many subtle, hopeless errors may be introduced. That little shed or garage or whatever that frame structure with the window is behind him seems a likely place to undertake such work. That seems exactly where you go to labor deep into the night, away from family and distractions, to address such delicate matters that depend on deviations not exceeding some excruciating tolerance. There is nothing in his life—his job, his coming home and hanging about and kicking off his shoes and having dinner and paying attention to his wife and, if it's summer, going to bed with the windows open—to prepare him for such tolerances. The necessary poise and balance don't come so easily. The measured understanding he assumes must be available to others. Errors creep in—on the order of a millionth of an inch—before you know it. Think of that. In bed with the windows open—all the accidental sounds of everything out there. To have such fine concerns. The heat of your fingers touching the glass (instead of the wooden handle on the top) can screw it up as you are grinding. Glass, you know, expands with heat. What is that vine that climbs the shed? Surrounds the window? Makes a rustling sound sometimes when there's a breeze when he is grinding late at night? You make a mistake at work, at home, you usually know it right away. The slightest thing and you can tell. The tone of voice. A look. A silence. Things like that are nothing at all. You let it go. But here the error breathes upon it. Sighs and whispers back and forth with the abrasive. It's a marvel and a torment. One's own bulk involved in this. To think a millionth of an inch might be leaned into, shoved around. And then detected and regretted with such clarity. You only need a lamp, a shade with a pinhole, and a razor blade to check your work. That's crazy. But that's it. It's puritanical. True virtue always wanting. Imperfection inescapable. Default. You want to see? Well, no, you really don't. It's too precise. Too startling in a way. Out here in the shed. Such sensitivity. Out there in the world one's errors average out, disperse like piss in a pool. But here they are confined. Within the shed. The imperfection shines forth. There's this glow of revelation that requires you to get down on your knees at one end of the bench to see it. Bring your eye to just the right position, slide the blade in its little stand sideways into the cone of light, the pinhole light reflected back from the mirror mounted on its edge at the other end. And there it is. You see as God must see. Within the glow, the shadowy departure from the truth. It seems all nature all about him, all the ordinary, accidental life, gets by as best it can. But not out here in the shed. It breaks his heart. Why does it have to be a razor blade? As if it were a physical slicing open. Does he wince? He does. He winces. As the razor blade cuts into the beam as if it were an actual dissection, light laid open to reveal some dark pathology within it. Light itself in doubt somehow. Virginia creeper. That's what climbs the white board siding of the shed and makes a fluttery sound like moths against the window now and then whenever a little breeze comes up. When there's a pause in operations. Or when kneeling at the bench he holds his breath to keep his eye wide open straight into the light. There is a chance, each time, it's going to be all right. But then you find the spot. Your eye is filled with perfect understanding of the problem. What you're after is an even, luminous gray that looks dead flat, which is the way the perfect spherical concavity presents itself in the knife-edge test. That's what you want to get with basic grinding. With an astronomical mirror. A reflection of that ancient intuition of the world. That it is flat. Although it's not. We know it's not. And yet the sphere, the shallow section of a sphere, appears as flat somehow or other. Or it should were there not zones of aberration. Personal error. When he contemplates himself, his bulk, his own irregular roundness, he allows such thoughts sometimes. Or thoughts approaching these at least, toward something like this same regret. And yet how sweet the way the light departs at evening. After dinner, standing, watching at the window. How revealing and forgiving all at once. The raking light across the yard. And all the yards. Until the ragged unintendedness of every little patch of ground, of everything, shines forth just as it starts to close upon itself, to settle into shadow. Then it's all the same again. How sweet to sense the knife-edge moment as it passes into gray. Forgiven. Something like forgiven. Just like that. The world forgiven just like that. Did not the Puritans admit the possibility of grace? Might not a few more turns out there, a few more kneelings at the bench, bring everything around at last? Or close enough to let it pass into that final realm of polishing called "figuring." Parabolizing. Deepening that dead-flat gaze to focus on the heavens. What a fine and clear and difficult intention. Just to have it seems almost enough. To get it all set up. To understand the preparations. Sometimes stand out there in the broad daylight in the backyard and consider, just consider, what someone would think who walked up to that shed and peeked, hands cupped to the face, into that little window, into what should be the nothing much, the sad leftover darkness of an ordinary life, where ordinary things accumulate—the gardening tools, the boxes full of stuff not quite discardable. Old parts of things. Old nearly empty cans of paint and so forth. None of that, though. What is going on in there? It is an altogether different sort of dark in there. If he should suddenly die—keel over right here in the broad daylight in the backyard, all spread out, his coat flopped open, ample belly in its clean white shirt presented to the sky—it would mean something even then. What would they think? His things—his clothes, his shoes and socks and pants and clean white shirts and odds and ends and pictures on the wall— well that's all sad, of course, but clear enough, dispersible. But what about this stuff, they'd ask. Oh dear, his wife would say. Oh dear, and stand there looking in and shake her head and not quite know. Or not remember very clearly. Though he told her. For a telescope. A telescope? To have it in the yard. To bring it out when the weather's nice. When friends stop by in the eve- ning, say. Put out some chairs. Some light refreshments on a tray. They'll say, "My goodness!" "What in the world!" And shake their heads to hear him talk about the difficulties. So much time involved. And would they care to have a look? Of course they would. The tinkle of ice. The back-and-forth between the kitchen and the yard. The sound of ordinary talk resuming, un- perturbed as people break away to have a turn. A little awk- wardly. Like peeking through a knothole in a fence. Hands cupped to the eyes. They're not quite sure. You focus here. Just turn the knob. But they would rather not. They never want to turn the knob. Oh no, it's fine, they'll say. Though they have no idea. They'd rather not commit to more than this, get more in- volved than just this walking up and bending in toward some- thing pretty easy, incidental. "Oh, how wonderful." And not so far away. They've no idea. But surely not so far away.

2

YOU JOIN THE WORLD, SPREAD OUT TO FILL IT, STRETCH YOURSELF SO thin you nearly disappear when you're a child. You find yourself, at two or three or so, distributable, extendable—in physical fact, and principle—to any point within your understanding. Every place a place to go. You could be anywhere. Good Lord. Nearby—knelt down beside the cold concrete foundation of the house for no good reason, just to be there; or beside this bush; or upon this shaded patch of dirt; or out there in the distance (such a strange idea, the distance) where you know there must be places, dirt and bushes or their cognates. You could be out there as well—might be already in a way. Once you get going with this thing it's hard to limit. Once you lose the natural center of the world—all things inflowing, all directed toward the mouth—there's nothing keeping you. You spread out irretriev-

ably. Like spilt milk, as we say. For something lost. Beyond re-
gretting. I suppose it might have felt like that—a thinning out, a
tending toward translucence. If I try to place this feeling, or this
notion of a feeling, in that flat and treeless moment in Fort
Worth where my first thoughts occur, or memories of thoughts,
it's like playing some strange modernist score behind a silent
movie. Sure it works. But is it meaningful—beyond the mere
dramatics? Are the mere dramatics meaningful?

To start with there's this little concrete porch that seems to
present me to the earliest ponderable state of things. Attached to
a little red brick house in a little postwar neighborhood more
bleak and flat and treeless—I have photos—even than the one,
the Dallas one, that followed where I would cut myself in the
alley on a deep blue piece of broken Noxzema jar. But this is it,
right here on the porch, at the point where, calculating backward, the equations all break down. The concrete porch that
makes no sense. Where sense begins. Where love and terror,
only recently emerged as separate forces, aren't yet capable of
complex interaction. Things have barely opened up, resolved as
things—first things, I think—and then as places. So now you're
lost as soon as found. You could go anywhere, be anywhere
among the possibilities. Out there on the lawn, the dry Bermuda grass as vast and featureless as steppe; across the street
where such a glare comes off those thoughtless little boxy white
frame houses in the afternoon it hurts to think of being there, to
sense yourself available, transferable out there into that light, that
awful clarity of things, of house and ground and empty sky. The
pure unmediated facts.

I want to think all this might constitute a pretty fair experiment. An only child presented to what seemed almost unbearable simplicities. Deriving not from any deprivation but from circumstances following the war—the sudden need to reestablish the conditions of our lives for those returning. There's no time to think about it. It just happens. (Telescopic views from space, from other worlds, would have disclosed faint rectilinear expansions into regions formerly empty.) Here you had an understanding of what structure life required. Unquestioned. Any first-grade kid could draw it: house and grass and sky. But actually built like that—as if from crayon renderings. Abrupt and thoughtless. All these sudden postwar children popped into these sudden postwar neighborhoods at once. You're not going to get a clear and simple reconstruction of the world like this too often. Pay attention. Hold the moment, from the cold gray concrete porch, as long as possible. Take time, as you grow older, to recover and maintain whatever data seem reliable. That feeling— it's all feeling, thoughts are feelings—that the world receives you at a certain cost. There's an exchange involved. As soon as you are specified, you're lost. Somehow or other. There is heartbreak. Can one possibly have felt it? Does it constitute a thought? Can one get back there to the porch, to clearest terms, and recognize it like a smell retained but never quite identified till now? A sad suspicion. Write it down. It sounds like some weird rule of physics. You can be here or you can be special. But not both.

3

I CAN REMEMBER WATCHING BULLFIGHTS ON TV WITH MY GIRL-
friend's semi-invalid mother in the late sixties. Seems to me it
was some oddball local channel—UHF 39, I think—providing
untranslated coverage from Mexico of action in the provinces
quite late on Saturday nights. Like they'd run out of everything
else and who'd be watching at that hour anyway. Just me and
Deborah's fading mother in her wheelchair, I imagine. Certainly
no one else in the family. Nor, I'm pretty sure, in all that almost
uniformly white North Dallas neighborhood. My goodness,
what is this? they would have said before retiring, clacking man-
ually through the channels for some last little bit of local news or
weather. Staring a moment at the terrible, fuzzy, awkward pause
and lurch of it. Like amateur pornography. Too real. Too strange.
Not how we like to think of it at all.

She suffered from some neuromuscular disorder, I believe. Progressive, wasting. Yet occasionally relenting. She required injections often and, since I was better at it and less squeamish than the others, it would fall to me whenever I was there. We'd started poorly. As a college senior I was perceived to have been the one to introduce her freshman to the permissions of that era. A perception I was sworn by Deborah never to correct. However, I came to find a certain satisfaction, a nobility, in taking on the guilt in a symbolic, theological sort of way. And sometimes standing in the kitchen before the bulletin board of honor—whereon every commendation and certificate of achievement ever conferred upon three high-performing children, every badge and ribbon ever awarded were displayed—and keeping my allegorical distance. I'd no honors. Never so much as a star on the fridge. But, then, what need had I? Was I not Fate? The shadow upon such glories?

What inspired the bullfight thing I can't recall if she ever said. Perhaps she'd traveled south in her youth and seen such things. Perhaps read Hemingway or Lea. But there she was one Saturday night—I'm guessing Saturday; guessing channel 39; the wheelchair; she may not have been in the wheelchair yet, though she was very frail—but there she was, intent, involved. What is that? Bullfights. No. Yet sure enough. I took a seat. I see it now in black and white, and grainy like old photographs. But live. Obscure but vividly obscure. The clumsy rudiments to that glamorous sweeping gesture shown in posters, velvet paintings. This would not transcribe to velvet very well. Would not hang happily in restaurants. Above your enchiladas, might discourage conversation. Yet she knew to look for moments. Anything approaching grace in these entanglements, bewildered confrontations at the margins of the art. And now and then, for an instant, it would come together—lesser matador and lesser bull would find, somehow, the greater understanding and you'd glimpse that massive lunge into the emptiness, the swirl. Oh, look, she'd whisper. And I would, as best I could. Make mental notes. Attempt to join the connoisseurship. Death is air. Within the swirl. The massive fact evaporates within the tossing of the cape. Right? Nothing to it. That's the whole idea. Right? Why the matador is all got up in golden sparkles? Can't, in principle, be touched. He is abstract. Immortal. Never mind how messy it can get. There *is* a principle involved. Out there on the margins, in the dirt. Where myth arises, don't you think? She'd let me ramble on. I guess she liked the company. My theological insights.

You mustn't try to be polite with the needle. Don't be kind, reluctant, making a face and feeling it yourself and terribly sorry about the whole thing every time. It needs to be a mere formality. A knock on wood. The sign of the cross. Like a dart. Not letting go, of course. But quick like that. And thoughtless. Somewhere down the line it's life or death, but not today. A swab, the smell of alcohol, a hazy summer sky.

Not thirty years before the bullfight sessions, Deborah's neighborhood was cotton fields. Before that, tallgrass prairie. Even now it feels exposed. As all the sudden postwar neighborhoods out here. That I keep dwelling on. Sweet diagrams. A few, like Deborah's—just a little west of the housing boom and all that grand and complicating verticality—still pretty much pristine. Though threatened, certainly, like pristine tallgrass prairie, only patches of which remain, protected. Pristine prairie remnants, they are called. And greatly valued—for the density and rarity of plant and animal species and, I have to think, for keeping us in mind of how it was, of where we were, still are in a way. How close above these sudden, pristine little neighborhoods the hazy summer sky, the empty air, descends.

First come the picadors, the mounted lancers. Classically two—who try, as other toreros test the bull with their capes, to strike him right at the base of the neck to wound him slightly, bring his head down, get his attention. In the old days horses might be disemboweled. But now the mount is well protected. Still it seldom goes very gracefully or accurately. Immediately you think, Oh crap, this doesn't look too good. All the formality, the gorgeous glittery pose, breaks down—is always at the verge of breaking down—into a scramble. Run and scatter. Back to basics. And yet somehow recomposes. Unembarrassed. As if ritual were more basic still—the truer state of things. Condensing naturally out of terror. There is something indecent here. Beyond the simple physical cruelty. (You glance away from that—not hard; the picture's pretty fuzzy out of Juárez or wherever.) It has something to do with ritual retaining unabsorbed and untransformed its crude originating impulse. All those glittery priestly figures should be swirling around and poking at some gaudy representation far removed from huge and bloody primitive facts. What seems indecent is the ritual half-formalized, half-dressed—its awful structure right out there for all to see.

I think I tended to lean back a bit. Away from the actual point of it—the placing of the lance, and then the flinging of the nasty barbed and dangly banderillas and, of course, at last, the sword. Good grief, the sword. A fragile tiny-hilted hypodermic needle of a thing. How could it possibly be useful, much less merciful? The bull will not go down. And so you have to do it again and maybe again—the way a child will pick at an injury. Stop doing that. But somehow we can't help it. We keep going for that clear, indecent glimpse into the interval, the gap.

I think of her, now, reduced to this. I didn't think so much about it at the time. But now I think, I feel, that she must have sensed this critical indecency. How others in the family left her to it. As to an IV or some other drawn-out automatic medical procedure. I'm okay with the indecency, however. I've no honor. In a little while I'll probably leave with Deborah. But for now I am allowed this station here with her. She's dying. It won't be for years but, still, she is. And here she's watching bull-fights. On this little TV in black and white, in Spanish, in the middle of the night—what feels like the middle of the night—and in the middle of this pallid tallgrass prairie of a neighborhood.

Is ritual inevitable? The truer state of things, condensing naturally out of terror? As a photographic image seems a natural condensation. Just as meaning, for that matter. You just have to pay attention. Everything is poised to represent another thing, another possibility. The air, the empty air, is full of meaning. Did you know that the dapples of sunlight under a tree are blurred and overlapping images of the sun? Not just the wash of light, like water, leaking through. But actual photographic images—a repetitious murmuring. The sun, the sun, my God the sun in a sort of whispered chant beneath the pinhole camera gaps among the leaves. In an eclipse you see it easily and marvelously as all the intermingled roundish patches go to crescents.

In *The Brave Bulls*, Tom Lea's novel, Luis Bello, famous matador who's lost his nerve, regains it at the end. "The fear that drained away from Luis Bello's heart . . . seeped strangely outward through the sand, past its rim, up through the stands of the plaza, into the heart of the crowd." I think of Deborah's mother at the center of a similar formality—or, rather, an extension of that terrible schematic. Terror gathers at the margins of the ritual, escapes through gaps, through clumsiness or fearfulness out there at the very edges, breaking free of the containment. Filling the little TV screen, irradiating Deborah's mother. And from there seeps out into the night, into the sleepy neighborhood, sweet diagram of us, into the hearts of couples lying in those carpeted and curtained sixties bedrooms where they turn away from one another, wakeful in the dark as, through the curtains, filtered flickerings of passing headlights move across the ceiling and the walls.

4

YOU SENSE THE INTERVAL, THE CLEAR EXPECTANT EMPTINESS BE-tween things in the fall. In early fall as it is now. The first cool weather brings a feeling of the air gone slack as if, itself, deflated and released from some supportive or expressive function we have gotten used to. All the usual little noises—children, lawn-mowers, barking dogs—seem suddenly singular and distant. Disconnected. And it's always a surprise. You walk outside in the morning, pause there in the driveway with the paper, all the clamor of the world contained therein, and think what's this? This cool withdrawal. Have I been out here before? With every-thing so opened up. The sounds of things all scattered out across the quiet. What is this? A change in the weather? Something's missing, for the moment. Some unstated understanding. Dog and lawnmower have no knowledge of each other. Things recede to a faint, perhaps remembered, picture-book simplicity. Each sound a simple question, one per page—what's this? And this? Can you remember? And you get this sort of longing—as for all these things dispersed and, for the moment, unavailable. As for the moment, somehow, unavailable. As for some moment past. Which seems to amount to a sort of longing for right here, right now—this very place and moment where you are. Is this what happens in the autumn when the first cool air arrives? Do we get wistful, every one of us all up and down the street— bewildered, doubtful, inexplicably nostalgic for the items of the present? For ourselves? How can that be? It makes no sense.

★

NORTHEAST OF HERE ARE SEVERAL TALLGRASS PRAIRIE REMNANTS. Years ago I made a trip out there with a friend who'd been before—who loves such things as vanishing prairies, antique roses, cemeteries. I suspect, as with my dead friend Doug, it has to do with a horrifying childhood and a sense of loss, of wound, as a sort of clearing. As providing a maintainable and valuable perspective. I had just begun a book about the idea of the past and thought the idea of a vast primeval grassland might be simi-lar in ways—in its absorbency, its blur of possibility. Which sounds more like the future, I suppose—but there you go. It gets confused. So, anyway, I was excited when she told me of these remnants that had somehow been identified, preserved. It took a while for her to find her way again. It is the nature of such places to be hidden. Overlooked. It's hard to remember, lacking GPS, the reference points—the ragged little towns, the turns down barely indicated county roads. And even then you run right past, so deep the sense of nothing much out here to see. That much remains. It is the quality of emptiness that's changed. But there it is, the deeper emptiness at last. Back up. Pull in and park. Consult the sign with a map that shows which portions of the acreage protected are restored and which unplowed, pristine—a fifty-two-acre patch as it turns out, an honest glimpse (as through a wrapping-paper tube) of ancient, boundless, wavy nothing much that always seemed, portrayed on television or in movies, crossed by settlers, desperadoes, as more hopeless than the sea.

I wonder why that special hopelessness. You'd think the sea, the Arctic waste, the desert, outer space were much more terrible. And yet, perhaps, less hopeless, in that hope might not be felt at all sustainable in these. In perilous circumstances. Thus its absence not a constant tugging at the heart. As in the tallgrass, one imagines, where the emptiness precedes and seems to guide you, open before you, even welcome you into it. Seems to receive you as a part of it. An implicating emptiness. Imagine desperadoes lost and horseless on the tallgrass blackland prairie. How their desperation rarefies, expands into the grass. Their violent temperaments exhausting and diffusing into the random, buzzing insect life around them. These would be the sort of men who, as they say, live in the moment. Men not given to reflection, here discovering the moment—vital, empty—unendurably extended. Slowly, slowly made aware—as the condemned in Kafka's story have the laws they've disobeyed inscribed upon their backs mechanically by delicate degrees—that it belongs to them. It can't be shaken off with wild behavior, mere belligerence. They're in it now. In for it. There is nothing to prepare them for a lostness, for a hopelessness like this. Perhaps they'll turn on one another after a while. Can you imagine just the sound of walking through tall grass like that—chest-high at least—for days and days? And if it's windy there's a sound to that as well. And all so gentle. Like a sigh. There should be hope in that, you'd think. You'd think a desperado, even, might allow some recollection of some distant, faded tenderness to join the general whisper of the insects and the grass. But, then, how hateful that might be. To sense himself, some secret dearest self, presented in this lostness. He's not ready for that. Nor, I suspect, am I.

But now it's fall. And out here standing in the driveway, in the interval the change in weather brings, there is a pastness to the present and a sort of tallgrass prairie of the heart. I think I probably ought to drive out there again. And take the risk.

My friend can't come this time. I've Google-Mapped the region. Made a copy. Marked the route in red. Disdaining GPS, I'd rather feel my way out to it. Have to consult this faintly printed little map crisscrossed invisibly by tiny county roads whose clearly printed tiny numbers float about like calculations, probabilities. Should I run out of gas, drift off the road into a ditch, set out on foot, get lost somehow, to be discovered, finally, not much left, bones bleaching inexplicably after only a week or so like those of some poor long-forgotten desperado (and, so tragically, no more than a couple of hundred feet from a strip mall or a trailer park, of which there are so many out that way)—but should that happen, they would find my little map, my clear intention. "Oh," they'd say, and pass it around. "Look, he was searching for the tallgrass blackland prairie of the heart."

And stand there quietly for a moment, faces flashing softly red in the squad-car lights like at the end of *West Side Story*.

Head out north on Highway 75 past endlessly reiterating mercantile development. There used to be a northern edge of town. It used to grade away to open field and pasture. But no more. I miss that feeling of departure. North is where we used to go when I was young, to find the country. To go shooting, drinking, build a fire and hang out with our girlfriends for an evening. Sense ourselves escaped, extended in a way—that way you sense yourself extended when you top a hill and find that the road swoops down and away for a thousand miles or so; though in this case, in the dead-flat dark with a bottle of something or other 1959 that this particular store would sell you for five bucks no questions asked, it was amazing; it felt less like miles than years spread out around us, running under all the shotgunned "Posted" signs, the plowed fields rippling out away from us forever.

At the town of McKinney take a right to the east on Route 380, through the smaller town of Princeton, to the even smaller town of Farmersville. Now you're in the country. You've departed all that other. But departure of the deeper sort is difficult. Northbound on 78 from Farmersville toward Blue Ridge, watch for County Road 825. I run right past on into Blue Ridge, turn around, and try again.

My friend Dr. Barron Rector, associate professor and extension range specialist at Texas A&M, tells me it's possible to spot, within the city—in the older parts especially, the vacant lots and alleys—shaggy, accidental residue of prairie. Micro-memory. Little patches. Fleeting glimpses here and there. No, that's not johnsongrass. That's something else. That's . . . what? What do you call that? If you get down on your knees there in the alley right next to it . . . listen, really, you can hear the wind like ocean in a seashell.

There it is. I make a U-turn. Come back to it. Goodness— sign about the size of a license plate. It's a formality. What business could you have out here and not already know which way to go? These little roads convey down narrow possibilities. Toward few and scattered points, among the fields, where sedentary life originates, condenses self-protectively as ever.

And again I drive right past. The closer you come, it seems, to nothing much, the harder to identify. Well, that makes sense, I guess. Suggesting maybe we're approaching that same quantum physics–sounding sort of problem as, way back there near the start of this whole thing, in that old photograph—so sad and so compelling—of the little girl in the swing in 1910 or so, in Omaha, Nebraska. How her face, so blank and open, blurring toward us in the swing, seems to present, out of that unresolvable photographic stillness, such a longing, such a strain toward us, the world, the here and now. Toward our belief and our receiving her, the fact of her somehow. And how the more we concentrate, attempt to come to terms, the more the fact recedes. The more her blankness overexposes, washes out into that pale expanse of weedy grass that fades away behind her all the way to the horizon.

Back up to it. No cars coming. No cars anywhere at all. I'd reimagined more than this—a small brown sign with "Parkhill Prairie" in white letters and a low steel fence. But here it is. Less fanfare than a produce stand. Turn in, pull round the circular gravel path, park near the dedicatory plaque and the explanatory signage, just beyond which there's an arbitrary-looking unprotected line where mown grass stops and tallgrass prairie starts. So, just like that. I had forgotten. How abrupt. Here is your ordinary ground, the ground you're used to—gravel, grass—and here your emptiness, a piece of that 250-million-acre emptiness that once extended all the way from Texas into Canada. This hard-edged presentation makes me think of James Turrell's constructed glimpses of the sky—his simple buildings where one sits to gaze up through a large square aperture so clean the structure reads as less substantial than the emptiness it frames.

Today the sky is low and gray, the wind substantial through the tall grass. Sudden gusts. I don't remember this before. I don't remember ever hearing quite this heavy, empty sighing. There's a mown path out into it. So I walk a little ways. I'll bet the sound of wind through corn or wheat is different. As it is through different trees. The wind through cottonwoods sounds just like running water, I have noticed on my walks about my neighborhood. The wind through different neighborhoods, in turn—if one could find a place sufficiently removed wherefrom to gain the broader sense of such a thing, as with a ten-mile line of saxophones—might give a certain insight into broader correspondences and meanings.

When I say the empty air is full of meaning, I suppose I mean its emptiness presents the possibility of meaning. Represents, in palpable form—as wind especially, dramatically, emphatically—the emptiness across which meaning propagates. The migratory distance between pasture, water. Points of temporary resolution. Of arrival. Where the desert smeared and airbrushed over the side of your 1970s van collapses and you're here—for a moment anyway, at campsites Acheulean, sub-Saharan, Yellowstonian.

Those sudden, diagrammatic postwar neighborhoods do feel a bit like campsites. Here we are, you see. We've settled in. Exposed like this, on treeless ground, to night and day and calm and wind and everything—it doesn't feel as if we plan to stay here very long. Just long enough to hold the thought. What thought? I think I've asked before.

Not far from the pallid postwar neighborhood where Deborah's mother liked to watch the bullfights is a remnant of an earlier and less confident incursion onto the cotton fields. Three insular two-block streets of rudimentary, trepidatious postwar housing. Here is where, in the sixties, my friend Vernon lived for a while with his mother and younger brother. It's unchanged. Somehow protected as encircled over the years by much more prosperous development. The way a tree will grow around an injury. So strange. And strangely windy, as it seems to me, back then. Which makes no sense. Cannot have really been the case, of course—a quality of windiness belonging to this particular spot. Yet that's what I remember, visiting Vernon. Usually late afternoon or evening. Dark and sparsely furnished living room transitioning to kitchen where, likely as not, on the kitchen table would be materials for discussion—books and projects. Astronomical, aeronautical. Once a balsa-wood propeller he had carved to a gorgeous sculptural translucency like something by Brancusi. And the wind. Through weather stripping. Humming, rising now and then into this saxophonic howl. And up and down like that all evening. Out of the north. All through the house. I think the house must have been very finely tuned to mournful tallgrass prairie frequencies. These moody, resonant silences into which our discussion tended to lapse. And here's the thing. They had this dog. His mother's dog. A Kerry blue terrier—maybe fifty pounds. A big one. Charlie. Crazy as shit. And always loose in the house—this shadow wandering around within the general humming and lapsing. Always ready to bite you at any moment for no reason. Try to pet him and he'd let you for a minute. Then he'd bite you. Snap his head around and let you have it. Damn. Drew blood one time. Yet there I was. I knew the risk. You'd think they could have put him up. But no. Somehow, he had to be there. You just had to watch your step. Not meet his gaze, make sudden moves. Be poised, deliberate, resigned. A velvet painting would portray me in dramatic chiaroscuro under the light above the table, starting gracefully to turn as, out of the velvet black, comes Charlie toward me—eyes and teeth and horns.

So here's a ritual. A cruel initiation. (Can it ever not be cruel?) Involving a darkened room, the wind through weather stripping, rising and falling like bull-roarers or didgeridoos and in the room somewhere, forever, is this dog.

In a book of essays I wrote a number of years ago there's a photograph of dead-straight white caliche road through scrubby nothing much outside San Angelo. Dead straight and flat right out to the horizon—which I'd estimate to be about a thousand miles away. I'm thumbing through for something else but stopped by that. And that grass that grows beside the road in windy clumps and looks like remnant fundamental emptiness to me. Not tallgrass maybe, but some lower grade of emptiness. Old dirt or caliche roadsides, Barron Rector tells me, may here and there retain "historical" grasses. Now I wish I'd thought to kneel down close and listen in the wind. Which was so heavy on that day an empty rifle cartridge, found there on the ground, would whistle when you held it up. ("How windy was it? It was so windy you could hold an empty rifle cartridge up . . .") That road leads out into the emptiness where a rancher stalked a diabolical coyote that eluded all his skills, would not be snared or called and had, for two years running, killed his lambs. But finally, having made his camp out there on a hill one night, he lured it out of the predawn gloom with the tape-recorded cries of his infant daughter. At a hundred yards, a single shot from a brand-new rifle never fired again. And the world is saved. The lambs and—in some sense, as sense expands out here to fill the space—the crying baby and the rest of us as well. And to this day the natives gather at the appropriate time to remember and to reenact. To hold the empty cartridge up and listen to it whistle in the wind.

The sky falls in and you get animals. Frazer tells how it is common in parts of Europe, whenever the wind is seen to move across the corn, for the peasants to say, "The Wolf is going over, or through, the corn," "The Rye-wolf is rushing over the field," "The Wolf is in the corn," "The mad Dog is in the corn," and so on. In addition to whatever understanding of the agrarian world this represents, it serves to discourage children from venturing out into the fields to pick the beautiful deep blue cornflowers growing there. In Van Gogh's *Wheatfield with Cornflowers* you can pretty well infer, within the turbulent wheat and the tossing flecks of Noxzema blue, the wolf, the mad dog, or whatever.

It's about five miles to the east from Parkhill Prairie to Clymer Meadow, a larger tallgrass prairie remnant. I've not been there, but I've marked it on my faintly printed map. There is a website offering access by appointment but my calls were not returned. So I'll just drive by, have a look. This feels so much like when I drive through childhood neighborhoods of mine. I have no business here. No practical concerns. I look suspicious. Slowing, rolling down the windows, taking pictures. If you didn't know, you wouldn't think a thing just driving by. A field of grass. Untidy pasture. Acreage lapsed. A rusting pickup truck would not seem out of place. Abandoned farm equipment. What do you call those ranked steel disks the tractor pulls across the field to break it up? To furrow it. A harrow? I should know this stuff. My father's people mostly came from farming people. You could hear it in his voice from time to time. When he got angry, you could hear his father's father—or before that, way before that maybe, yelling out across some field by Brueghel. He could whistle through his teeth in that ear-shattering way appropriate to calling distant animals. To children, though, terrifically alarming. Where does that come from, I'd wonder, in so kind a man? My misbehaviors suddenly belonging, as it seemed, to a broader class of violation than I understood. I doubt he understood.

Disc harrow. That's what that is called. That terrible thing. In Kafka's story it's the "harrow" that inscribes the violation on the backs of the condemned. Or, more precisely, the injunction violated.

I could sometimes gain a clearer sense of origins whenever we'd drive south to visit Great-granduncle Oscar near the tiny town of Palmer in an old two-story white frame house with a barn out back, into whose hayloft one could climb to throw things—sticks and things—down into the chicken yard to get them all excited. Words and expressions were used that seemed, to me, unusual and possibly archaic.

When Uncle Oscar died, we gathered in the small and somewhat brutal little turn-of-the-century Baptist church in Palmer. At the conclusion of the service we filed out and there he was right by the door. They'd wheeled him out into the vestibule—I guess you'd say the vestibule—right there as we were passing into the glare of the afternoon. And such a glare. A hard, flat light that came off dusty asphalt street and gravel parking lot. It filled the little vestibule and shone on Uncle Oscar. I had never seen the dead before. I thought there seemed to be a sort of glaze or something to it. Semigloss if it were paint. A yellowish beige. And very uniform. How odd to have him brought right up to the edge of the afternoon with us, to the point of our departure—no transition; you could hear the crunch of gravel right out there, the conversations starting up. I can remember very clearly, for some reason, as we left the church, my mother's high-heeled footsteps on the sidewalk. Squinting down to watch her stepping on or over the cracks and then onto the gravel. Why in the world should I retain a thing like that?

These little towns out here seem barely here, but stabilized as barely here. As tentative. As if, from the start, constructed toward a tentative idea. An idea, maybe, *of* the tentative. Which, I suppose, makes sense if you're a farmer. Life so spread out, after all, exposed to such a glare. The terrible contingency. When it was mostly cotton one could have one's parents stop by the side of the road to let one dash across the ditch to pick a boll to take back home to keep for years atop one's dresser as a souvenir of all that flat and ancillary life that seemed, so strangely, to impinge on ours at intervals. From way out there, so strangely. Linguists, trying to determine where the very earliest speakers of some ancient language came from, take what seem to be the earliest words and lay them out to see what they describe. I try to imagine what my father's simplest, harshest vowels and usages describe. He wouldn't like this. More than anything he wanted to be kind. And so he was. Yet I imagine an unkinder and more fundamental landscape. With more fundamental threats. Someplace wide open is my guess. Where words spread out and loosen up as if accompanying some physical exertion. Or to carry in the wind. Across the cotton or the sorghum or the corn. For generations down through southern states and out onto the Texas blackland prairie where the cotton liked to grow. Though not so much anymore, of course.

I think I thought death would be heavier. Less movable. Less easily shown, departed from. Less well illuminated. Less concise, perhaps, in a way. I think I thought—it's hard to know; you try to reconstruct toward something; you're interpreting yourself; translating, really, from what seems the ancient language of your childhood—but I think I thought, or no, not thought but felt or faintly sensed, that death had coalesced, had formed itself like a pearl from these conditions way out here. That these conditions might be favorable in ways that those obtaining in my life at home were not. An altogether simpler process so far out upon the openness, the barbed-wire-stitched-together continuity of things—not really so far out, just thirty miles or so, but going south you lose the city pretty quickly—where there's not much to impede or redirect or complicate the broad dispersion of our longings and our sympathies which, I suspect, released like that, must always have been tentative, diffuse and understood to be re-gatherable, compressible, at last, into this simple presentation, barely separated from us, all aglow in the reflected afternoon.

I have been paging through a family genealogy my father had prepared. And once you get past introductions and the phony coat of arms, you have these photocopies—much deteriorated from repeated iterations, passings forward of the rumor—of old photographs of stolid family groups. Then all these names. So many names. So many vestibules. I find I tend to squint at these old images—run through so many copyings of copies that the boost in contrast reads as glare, the information coarsening as if somehow eroded by the scrutiny, unable to withstand it. Rendered doubtful, almost. Tentative. Provisional. We think there were these people and they looked like this—at least when made to stand or sit together for a moment. Otherwise they tend to blur into the general migration of the ancient vowels and usages across the vast exposure of the Russian steppe, some scholars have proposed, down into Europe, central Asia, and beyond. And on out here, just barely here at last, sustained in these conditions out of which we all resolve. Out of the distance and the emptiness and glare.

PART THREE

1

I HAVE A PICTURE OF BETTY CROCKER ON MY DESK. A FIVE-BY-SEVEN black and white that's nicely framed in matte aluminum. Who's that, my younger friends will ask. Oh, where shall I begin.

First off, you'll notice it's enlarged from a halftone image—from some 1950s magazine ad, I guess. And it's inscribed at upper left: "To David, with gratitude for your steadfast support." And signed at bottom right: "Love, Betty." That last hard to see against the dark gray of her dress which, in the contest-winning painting that established her new image in 1955, is red.

"Which Betty Crocker?," Nancy phoned to ask one evening not long after our occasional conversation had begun to expand somewhat beyond the school lacrosse fields where our daughters played, and after Nancy had been made aware of certain of my charming eccentricities including my insistence upon and devotion to the physical and spiritual reality of the advertising figure Betty Crocker in her serial manifestations. "Which one?" Nancy wanted to know. Which best expresses her? Which era? Oh, well—nineteen fifty, nineteen sixty. Right in there, I think.

So a week or two later there's a package on my desk. Inside is Betty. Framed. The right one too. Exactly the one I had in mind. So clear and kind of gaze. Serene with just the faintest touch of doubt, of sadness, at the edges of her smile. Her short perm, graying at the temples, modest, practical yet soft enough to ruffle, one imagines, in a warm breeze through an open kitchen window in those days of open windows in the summer. And that white wing collar. Pure and lily-like against the gray I know is red, and yet receptive to the breeze, to our humanity, our feelings, curling open just an inch or two beyond the prim and proper you'd expect. She's poised, deliberate, resigned. Exactly what she needs to be as special nourisher and keeper of the hearth. And the inscription—Oh my God, that's perfect. "Steadfast." That's so perfect. That's exactly it. "Steadfast." So sweetly, sadly passed from beyond that cool, indifferent veil of halftone dots to me.

What can it mean? What sort of sentiment, what thought is represented here? If it were just a joke—had Nancy thought it merely that—she would have put it in some silly, gaudy Walmart frame, replaced the happy, general-purpose photographic moment such frames come with (to encourage us, to hold a place for happy possibilities) with Betty. Instead, it's a simple, flat, rectangular rim of anodized aluminum. This, then, is serious business, it would seem. She is resigned, on our behalf, to the eternal preparation. Is it done yet? Is it here? The here and now drawn out unbearably. She urges calm and faith that things will work out if you follow the directions. Take your time. She takes the place of general-purpose possibilities so easily. She slips right in. As thin as they. Or maybe even thinner. Photocopied halftone copy of a photograph. A step or two from vanishing, she needs a serious frame like this to fasten her in place.

★

CAN'T YOU IMAGINE CIRCUMSTANCES WHERE A SILLY, GAUDY WALMART frame is bought and taken home and found acceptable, for a while at least, as is? Happy moment already there. Ready to go. What's wrong with that? A person thinks. A somewhat desperate person, maybe. Hinging out the little easel stand and pausing for a second. Setting it down on the kitchen table. Standing back. What's wrong with that? It brightens the room. Compared to what she had in mind. Which wouldn't fit without some trimming. And a sense of obligation. Even loss. Whereas this moment—framed, installed as if belonging to her—beams in out of nowhere. Like a gift. A happy moment she'd forgotten. Loved ones lost and rediscovered in a way. The way you rediscover things you had forgotten all the time. Such happy moments must occur that, for some reason, are forgotten. And a thing like this, if not exactly those, can nonetheless be felt to stand for them. To hold a place for them. That's what they're for. Is that just crazy? Who's to say? Who pays attention?

★

NOW AND THEN WHEN FLIPPING THROUGH THE TV CHANNELS, I'LL GO past some cooking show and almost always turn back to it. (I am always running past the things that matter.) Almost always there will be, as part of the set, a window there somewhere behind the presentation. And I feel I need to check it out. (And always just the cooking shows—the sets of soaps or sitcoms hold no interest.) I require to know the realness or the falseness of the window. Not so easy anymore. And if it's false, a prop, to see if there's yet something of that strangeness I remember from the cooking shows of yore—that faint discrepancy between the real, material inner comforts of the kitchen and the world as merely gestured toward. That represented openness. The phony sky beyond the phony tree. I know. It's all so slight, so subtle. Must those intuitions that feel the deepest always, at the same time, feel so thin? They slip right into the gaudy frames we have for them.

These cooking shows create, it seems to me, a quality of hope and expectation not unlike what the religious shows intend. Look what we bring to you. Such comfort. Reassurance. Though, in this case, so immediate and real. As seemingly real as the gorgeous edibles in the earliest European still life paintings—which is what the TV cooking shows approximate, emotionally, I think. See what is possible. Available. Such kindness and abundance—here and now. A here-and-nowness that, in the late sixteenth and early seventeenth centuries, as painting sought to escape its ancient contract with religion, was regarded as encouraging so perilous an attraction to the pleasures of the world that, for a while at least, a warning seemed required as on a pack of cigarettes—a wilting grape leaf or a wormhole in the apple. Less explicit than the skull or the hourglass, but still enough to let you know the dangers of flipping down the channels in this way.

That food is real and really cooking on those cooking shows. Those are the actual cooking sounds. The actual sounds of chopping, frying. Were you on the set you would experience, beneath the imposition of the cameras and the lights and everything, the smells, the steam, the ordinary clear, anticipatory sense of it. Just as you would at home. As in the ordinary world. As cooking somehow seems to concentrate the world. Return it to its deepest center—all inflowing toward immediate desire. Oh boy. Oh boy. We are reminded how it all comes down to that. What do we have here—and they'll tell you. And they'll show you. In detail. For you should know. You want to know. Each thing, as in a still life painting, understood with great precision: this and this (the things we love) prepared/presented in this way exactly here, exactly now. Oh boy. It brings us into such a sweet proximity—the cooking show, the still life. All the best things of the world. But then your eye drifts to the wilt, the rot; the gentler, less specific admonition of the window.

Martha Stewart, in the images available online, stands in her kitchen on the set, before a window that, above the sink, looks out upon a gently rolling countryside. How strange, the way the almost-realness of it, the uncertainty (they've managed to contrive a sort of parallax; the view will shift a bit as cameras take a different angle)—but how strange the almost-realness seems to deepen the discrepancy. Which may be why that sorrel soup— that relatively simple preparation (season 4 of her "Cooking School") looks so appealing. As against that thin, yet somehow deep uncertainty out there. I'd like to have a bowl of sorrel soup myself. Such consolation, resolution, I imagine, in a bowl of sorrel soup.

There's what I guess you'd call an introductory shot to season 4 of *Martha Stewart's Cooking School*—with Martha posed behind a marble counter piled with vegetables of many kinds and colors. It's a perfect sixteenth-century representation of abundance. As presented in Vincenzo Campi's painting *The Fruit Seller,* circa 1580. And, like that, preliminary to the closer, finer apprehension of these things. The actual cooking, actual painting of desirable particulars. The images are practically identical. Here's Campi's ample vendor, sack of peaches overflowing into her lap, extending a bunch of grapes from her seat behind the baskets, bowls, and platters piled with every imaginable product of the garden and the orchard. She personifies, with peachlike cheeks and open blouse, the range of worldly pleasures, while behind, to the right, we're given a somewhat sketchy, hazy glimpse of the distant, hilly natural world itself. As if to remind that this is not a dream. A heavenly promise. But an actual demonstration of the things we love. And their availability. In principle.

And, so remarkably, much the same with Martha. Only a little more constrained, composed. And she, herself, too practical for allegory. Yet she stands in much the same relation to this bounty, all the produce of the season sorted—just as in the painting—into baskets, bowls, and various tidy heaps. And there to the left, behind it all, the view onto the faint, unconcentrated world beyond. The world halfway to nothing. What in the world is that about?

Within a very few years of Campi's "market picture," the first pure, "autonomous" still life paintings liberate the objects of desire from narratives sacred and profane. It's like the repeal of

Prohibition. Here is what we really want. We've always wanted. Since antiquity, when such depictions commonly adorned the greater houses of Pompeii and Herculaneum. For a thousand years we've known. And they appear like Christmas morning. Caravaggio's *Basket of Fruit,* circa 1595—dead-on, eye-level, child's eye-level, bright but absolutely empty background, basket right at the edge of the table, hanging over slightly. Grab it. Pull it toward you. As a child might, it suggests. It wouldn't take very much to tip it, flip the whole thing into your lap.

I can remember, at age six or seven, trying to draw a diamond. Not in order to have drawn it, but—in some hopeless sense not clear to me—to have it. Almost have it. Bring the idea of it closer. See, I've always been like this. It was about this time, or maybe a little later, having gathered a small collection of cheap, gold-colored metal trinkets—single cuff links, earrings, and such—and having considered, then embraced, the possibility that these poor things might actually be gold, that I persuaded my father to have one of his warehouse workmen melt it all down with an oxyacetylene torch. Into a single precious mass of solid gold, as I imagined. Though the result, of course, was an anti-alchemical puddle—all the glitter burning off immediately, pieces slowly slumping into the slaggy, leaden melt. There on the concrete in the bright blue afternoon. Why should I always seem to have gone at these things backward? Get the look right, first. Then see if the angels come. I think, however, that the drawing of the diamond might present the clearest case. The best experiment in meaning understandable as longing.

I'm pretty sure it was blue-ruled notebook paper, the kind we had in first or second grade, with nearly an inch between the lines to hold our huge and floaty thoughts in place. I'd got that standard diagrammatic diamond from a magazine ad or somewhere—trapezoidal top, triangular bottom. Try to get the zigzag facets right—with one of those awkward giant pencils everyone seemed to have back then. I'm at the dining room table. Dark outside. It must be getting pretty close to bedtime. I will do this. Blacken certain facets, leaving others bright to get the flash. The brilliant fact of it. Amazing. This will almost be a diamond. I will carry it to sleep. And in the morning have a look to see if meaning still inheres. If there's still hope.

Looking at Caravaggio's *Basket of Fruit,* you think: That's it. That's all you need to know. All still life painting after this is simply playing out the hand. Here is your love, your loss (the wilting leaf, the wormhole in the apple), the implicit invitation. This will do. But there's another step to take before it takes itself for granted as a genre and diffuses down the ages to become my mother's hobby. We step off into a deep dark place with the still life paintings of Juan Sánchez Cotán.

The even, golden light behind the *Basket of Fruit* goes dark. Dead black beyond the open gray stone window wherein vegetables and fruits and birds are placed, sometimes suspended. Brightly, clearly lit as prizes in some carnival game. And, in that bright immediate way, presented as immediately desirable, accessible. And all the brighter against the admonition of that uninflected dark beyond the window. And that dark is always there beyond the deep, gray, cold stone window. All the paintings— six surviving—are the same in this regard. And probably all from about the same time as the only one that's dated: 1602. Are we to understand that dark as night? If so, what is that brilliant raking light that looks like daylight? Broad daylight upon these things. As if these things bring light upon themselves. Bring all the light upon themselves. The world thus concentrating in these objects of desire. Reduced to this. And all that guilt, for all those centuries attaching to the world, released, subsumed into that dark out there. That greater, simpler mystery.

2

IT'S MAY. UNSEASONABLY WARM. I'M STANDING IN THE BACKYARD BY the rusty, frayed, and perforated trampoline, so irresponsibly left out here years after my three kids have grown, departed. Finally. Really. And, in one case, irretrievably, unimaginably. It's a danger now. An open well. A mine shaft. An "attractive nuisance." Clearly prosecutable. I'm waiting for the dogs to eat their supper, do their business; and considering how the sun, at five o'clock in the afternoon, comes through the higher "pinhole" gaps among the leaves of the pecan tree, casting fluctuating dinner plate–sized images of the sun onto the ground. They shift and dissolve and re-form as the branches sway in the breeze. I'm sort of hypnotized. Sometimes when the breeze picks up, a very clear yet fainter image manifests among the others. Isn't that strange. The sun, the sun, my God the sun. As if we need to be reminded, gazing down at the mostly grassless dirt by the trampoline. As if it were a thing we might lose sight of were it not for these projections. Unstill photographs. We think there is this source of light up there. This object up there in the sky that looks like this. That comes and goes.

A few weeks back, the black twelve-foot-diameter mat of the trampoline was covered with white catalpa blossoms. Perfectly, evenly distributed—these delicate little flowers. Like some ritual had taken place. A blessing performed. A peacefulness invited to descend upon such crazy, risky childhoods, which, with luck, some may survive. Up to a point, of course. Our unpredictable apogee.

My younger daughter's dog, a little dog that now, heartbreakingly, is mine, loves more than anything to chase the ball. The ball, the ball, my God the ball. It's all she wants to do. She is fulfilled. She thinks about it all the time. I think about it, too. Though not as much as she. "Hey, Penny. Where's your ball?" Her ears prick up. She scampers off to find it. Waits by the back door madly spinning counterclockwise till I open it. I wonder, if transported to Australia, say, she'd spin the other way. She waits to receive the toss or kick (the kick is quicker, more exciting, less predictable) with one foot up like a pointer. Tensed and focused. There is nothing else. Just this in all the world.

My mother—reader of Blavatsky, Yogananda, and Gibran—felt that dogs might be loved toward possession of a soul. A rudimentary sort of consciousness by contagion. Petted, spoken to, encouraged toward reflection of a kind. I am a dog. At last. And present in the moment. Although disinclined to see my own reflection in a mirror. That would be too much. Immediately having found myself to find myself displaced.

Betty Crocker, tell me, if you know. What keeps us here within the moment unendurably prolonged. Within the frame. There must be something coming, right?

Well, Penny thinks so. She is ready. In position. There is nothing like the strain of it. She shares my daughter's birthday. How about that. She shares as well, perhaps, in moments such as this, a certain emptiness. A longing for the arbitrary thing. Perhaps that thing my younger daughter seemed unable to discover in her mirror though unable to turn away. Please bring it. Kick it. Let me have it. Let me not be caught out here completely open to the wider empty world.

3

IT'S EARLY JUNE NOW. WE'RE IN ITHACA, NEW YORK, WHERE NANCY'S daughter's family moved about three years ago. Young Theodore is four. He has a sister who is one. These days I push him—them—about in a plywood spacecraft I constructed. They live on a twenty-acre farm, so lots of space.

Shall we be lost in space today? Shall we appropriate the vertical to horizontal purposes? Or possibly the other way around? And shall we pack our lunch and bounce along the path his father mowed through all that tall grass out into the wider emptiness? I think about that emptiness, my younger daughter's final understanding of it, fluctuating dinner plate–sized rumors of the sun projecting through it. Have you ever heard of a pin-hole camera, Teddy? He has not, so I construct one out of a shoe box. I decide to test my assumption that the very large size of the somehow sadly shifting, dappling images of the sun that I observed beside the trampoline that afternoon was due not to the size of leafy apertures but rather to the "focal length"—the height above the ground of the many-pinhole-forming canopy of leaves. Let's see. First cut rectangular openings at either end of the box. One to be covered with black plastic from a frozen-food container pierced, by means of graded needles from a sewing kit, with graduated apertures. From tiny to tinier to tinier still to barely enough to let the photons through. About an inch apart in a line across the middle. At the other end, a translucent screen of printer (once called typing) paper. Put the top back on and there you go. But too much general glare just holding it up to the sun like that. The eye shuts down. So, make like Mathew Brady, famous Civil War photographer, under a heavy black cloth focusing hood behind his great box camera. But instead of ghastly, patient long exposures of the dead, we get the sun. Four little suns through different apertures—one, two, three, four— beneath a dark blue towel. Oh, this is fine. The towel works fine. Why do I actually seem to feel like Mathew Brady? Maybe generally. Do I tend in that direction? Am I making too much of it? Under a hood and trying to focus on the sunlit dead strewn out across some battlefield. And trying to get the whole field in, achieve that depth of field, that depth of focus that requires the smallest aperture and thus less light and thus more time which, after all, we have. Why did those images of the sun upon the ground beside the ruined trampoline that afternoon seem sad? The dappled field of them.

Look, Teddy. Look. Come under the towel. Four suns. You see? Four little suns. And if we allow for increased blur with increased aperture, they're all the same size. Right? I am ful-filled.

The spacecraft I built about a year ago of quarter-inch ply-wood panels joined by small steel corner braces into a boxy fu-selage with a wedge-shaped nose. A sort of delta configuration at the rear—small tail on top and plywood wings that fold up out of the way for storage or reentry. And below the open view-port, a control panel with three toggle switches lined up at the left, and on the right a throttle lever. Space in the middle re-served for instrumentation yet to be imagined. And all set upon and fastened to a little four-wheeled garden cart they happened to have right there. At first to be pulled up and down the drive on careful taxi tests with Teddy in the pilot's seat and brand-new sister Rory, barely sentient, bouncing along like a bowl of gold-fish in the back; but later reconfigured by Teddy's scientist father to be pushed. An altogether superior system—with propulsion to the rear, where it belongs, and mystery forward, unobstructed. I had brought with me the instrument to finish the controls—a little oxygen pressure gauge from among the items left behind by the early rocket experimenter Robert Truax. Next to which I'd fastened a little silver plaque to explain that units here dis-played (of pounds per square inch) were convertible to miles or years or any real or imaginary quantity desired.

So now we're set. Our lunches packed and stowed, we're off—the two of us, along with Viva, the Australian cattle dog mutt as a sort of spirit guide, I guess—into that emptiness among the stars, along that path his father mowed. It makes a lovely sound—the plastic garden cart beneath the slightly teetery weight of everything. A pleasantly hollow, wobbly covered-wagon sort of sound as we proceed out of the solar system. Teddy spots a deer—a startled flash of white tail vanishing into the taller grass. What can we make of this? This *Alphaville*-like progress through the grass, as past those highway lights like stars between the galaxies? Shall we be able to hold these thoughts together? What's our pressure reading, Teddy? Gauge says zero. That makes sense, of course. Suggesting deepest emptiness. Whichever sort of emptiness. Oh, gosh. It strikes me sometimes, my sweet daughter, out of nowhere.

How about lunch? How about right here? We're near the halfway point. Not here, says Teddy. Over by that fallen tree. A few yards farther on. I am propulsion and narration. Not command.

So, what have you got? He stays in the ship. I'm standing, gazing down through the viewport while unwrapping my single slice of last night's pizza. Holy moly, what have you got there? It keeps coming out of the bag. It's like a magic trick: some Lebanon bologna, apple sauce in a spacey squeeze pouch, cheddar cheese, Ritz crackers, graham crackers—such a marvelous bounty, such abundance in such circumstances, little gauge at zero, deepest vacuum, deepest emptiness, yet look—strawberries, baklava (My goodness, is that baklava?), a bottle of lemonade.

As we approach the outer solar system, Viva spots a doe with fawn and instantly pursues. All disappear into the grass. I fear the worst—but pretty soon she's right behind us once again. And very happy for the chase. There seems to be an understanding.

★

GOING THROUGH MY YOUNGER DAUGHTER'S CHILDHOOD ARCHIVES—
boxed and stored away some twenty years ago—I find these four
remarkable drawings of the sun. Four little suns. Each on a separate white or pastel sheet of (typing/printer) paper. She's a little
younger than Teddy. I'd forgotten. They're extraordinary.
Sudden, as I recall. Emerging just like that out of the wild preconscious scribble-scrabble. All produced within a two- or three-
week span between October and November of 1988. The first
came home from her Montessori school—a yellow sheet with a
teacher's note at bottom: "Anna's Sun." Below which I have
added: "Anna Larwill Searcy Oct. '88." On palest yellow there's
this two-by-three-inch oval drawn in darker yellow marker. And
erupting from it all these multicolored, tangled, radiating lines
like hair on end, like cartoon startlement. A crazy, startled sun.
Surprised to be here. To be seen.

The next was done on plain white paper that same month
at the family tree farm in East Texas. In a little house by a lake.
So faint. So delicate in red and blue and yellow pencil—red for
the half-delineated roundness of the sun, for some of the radiating lines and for the face. A face emerges. Barely there but clear
enough. The radiating lines extend and sweep away to left as if
this sun has drifted into view against the breeze above the lake.
One eye looks back at us. Is this where this begins? Where everything, including us, looks back at us? One wants to know if
it is friendly. Happy. Sad. Bewildered maybe. Hard to say, just
barely visible as if she has to squint against the glare.

The third is terrible, explosive red and orange in heavy
marker radiating, detonating all across the pale blue sheet. I've
squeezed into the upper right her name and the date: 11-11-88.

And on the back I've noted that it was drawn at school. It's like she's suddenly looking through one of those hydrogen-alpha filters that astronomers use to peer into the roiling instabilities of the sun. The awful truth within that narrow slice of deep red light that renders all the weird magnetic turbulence, eruption—all the prominences and flares. Her ancient scribble-scrabble seems to reassert itself within the bloated disk to represent these violent forces that burst forth in countless radiating, twisting, sometimes knotting lines out to the very edge. It is alarming. Such a blaze of information from a three-and-a-half-year-old.

The last was drawn the following day at home on a sheet of plain white paper. It's a colorful, calm, composed, good-natured sun. It smiles upon us. Has two eyes, a nose, an upturned mouth. Our buddy the sun. No knowledge of that other. Squiggly rays in light and dark blue, green and red and yellow marker seem to represent that spectrum Isaac Newton demonstrated. But no matter. It's not science. Is it love? The sun, the sun. Might anything resembling love be love? Oh gosh. Was there such darkness in her even then? Such emptiness, the better to display these clear projections?

*

SINCE WE'VE VERIFIED THAT IMAGE SIZE INCREASES AS THE DISTANCE between the pinhole and the screen. And since we've got a lot of time on our hands out here. Since Viva doesn't seem so keen to chase the Frisbee anymore and I've run out of things to write about. And since the empty meadow seems to beckon from our upstairs bedroom window—I've decided to construct and to install out there a mighty pinhole camera of sufficient length to present a solar image large enough to reveal the presence of large sunspots, if there are any. Sound good, Teddy? What do you think of that? He's playing with his dinosaurs. That sound okay to you? I think it probably sounds okay.

A search produces a heavy four-foot cardboard mailing tube. Superb. A paper screen is taped to one end, sheet of aluminum foil with a nail-punched hole at the other. It's impossible, of course, to hold it steady, even to test. It needs support—a rickety six-foot stepladder, say, like that one out there in the garage (entirely suitable, experience suggests, for cardboard instruments of limited magnification)—and some sort of yoke on top to hold the tube in place while leaving it free to move about both axes. Up and down and side to side. What I come up with is an open wooden box with jigsawn holes in opposite faces to receive the tube. A miniature of Arcosanti's characteristic fenestrated cube, which makes me happy. This suspended so it rotates in a simple wooden fork, itself rotating about the single bolt that holds it atop the ladder. There you go. It remains to exchange the aluminum foil for graded apertures punched into numbered (one, two, three) Medaglia d'Oro coffee cans (of which there's such an accumulation out here in the garage as to have kept the previous tenant wide awake into the night, I have to think, to parcel out into each one the nails and bolts and brackets and fuses and every tiny useless, undiscardable part of his lonely life). Now, just to figure how to gather unto the viewing end that necessary darkness. Drapes are awkward. What about this plastic flower pot? I knock out the residual dirt and put it on my head. Oh yes, quite dark in here. I cut a hole, apply a lot of duct tape where it slides onto the back end of the tube and we are done.

It looks peculiar in the meadow. Like some higher-order scarecrow. But it works just fine. Just step right up and stick your head in there. Behold the sun. The size of a nickel. Number 2 aperture seems the best. So nice the way the cans slip over the end so easily. The texture of the paper is distracting. But it's pretty clear—no sunspots. There's a site online displaying current conditions on the sun. There are no sunspots. That's unusual, I think. Not one. So step right up and see the sun—abstract, inactive, perfect. Like a well-corrected mirror in that knife-edge test for optics. Now and then a cloud will cross and you can see it. Like a breeze among the leaves.

So when you die it goes like this. It all comes to you. All the arbitrary things—the ball, the sun, the glare itself, the glorious seasonal fruits and vegetables. It's all kicked back to you. It gathers in. It fills and completes you as the air fills up the tiny, noisy vacuum in the cicada. The stars wink out. And here's the strange part. You don't die, because the arbitrary thing you thought was you was never really there at all. At least not in the way you thought.

4

MARS HAS ONCE AGAIN COME INTO OPPOSITION—NEARLY AS CLOSE AS
it ever comes, quite low and bright between the trees in the
early morning, huge in the eyepiece and yet featureless as the
sun that day out there in Teddy's meadow. Mars gets these global
dust storms sometimes, we are told. But this is really one for the
books. So strange. At 640 power, nice clear disk, and nothing
there. Not even the normally brilliant pole. I paint some notes
and a very Zen-like empty circle. Three nights later just the
same.

A site online (as for the sun) presents the record, day by day:
high-resolution, image-processed photographs of Mars by amateurs from around the world employing all the best and latest
digital equipment and techniques. Even these are nearly blank.
It's not just me. One of these amateurs, I'm pleased to see, at-

tempts an actual drawing. I admire the struggle—still, he might as well have brushed a meditative *ensō*. Nancy ventures to suggest that the heavens, toward which I direct my world-averted gaze, have turned their gaze from me. So, now it *is* just me, apparently. All my fault. I try to displace myself, to glimpse myself, I guess, and look what happens. Like that dog in the mirror problem. It goes blank.

The higher power helps the glare, but nothing else. An even amber-yellow glare. If I stare long enough, I start to imagine Lowell's delicate tracery. As if that were default. What we return to.

As it happens, there's a relatively subtle dust storm blowing into Texas now from clear across the globe. A faint, attenuated plume from the Sahara turning skies a dingy yellow in the evenings with cicadas shrieking crazily—abnormally, it seems—in the heat and the weird, exhausted light. It feels a little like that 1956 approach—so ominous, impinging on us, I imagined then. So here again—the dust and heat and the hysterical cicadas. Mars impinges. Who can doubt it?

I have ordered a number 25 red filter—same as referenced in those ancient, hasty scribblings on the wall of Lowell Observatory. That's the one for Mars. Old number 25. For contrast and reducing glare. We'll see.

There is a pastness to the present. One has noted. One has felt. At times the distances between things seem historical. And therefore untraversable. As when, in early fall, you find yourself down there at the end of the driveway with the newspaper in your hand and can't get back. The distant children, dogs, and lawnmowers hold their places as de Chirico's deeply, metaphysically disconnected objects. And you can't get back. You can't just walk back up the drive toward—what? Toward where you were. You can't imagine a more purely empty interval than this. That vast and sad expanse of grass between the crippled subject of Andrew Wyeth's *Christina's World* and the farmhouse she is longing toward compares, perhaps, to this. Of course, all longing is the same. Although the intervals across which longing propagates have qualities. The untraversable Philippine mahogany scent of outer space. The smoky smell of early fall from down there at the end of the drive. The sweet, almost Gregorian chant of "Bette Davis Eyes" to fill whatever breathless distance. You have no idea, down there at the end of the drive, what's in the paper you are holding. It could be the Dead Sea Scrolls. The newsprint yellowing already. You have no idea what's happened in that distance up the driveway to the house. It takes your breath away. Not knowing. What to say about that distance? Pure and breathless concrete distance. At this moment. Everything, all history, drawn into it. You've seen how it goes as concrete sets. How easily, naturally, it receives impressions. Names, initials, children's handprints, tracks of passing animals—some possibly extinct. As if extinct. And, by extension, all the animals. The zebu and their herders. Clearly, such a concrete driveway is historical. Such concrete driveways have a special emptiness. All up and down the street in early fall. The first cool air, the faintest hint of smoke, we stand there for a moment with our papers far from home.

What is the quality of interval between us and the planet Mars? The Quality of Interval. Sounds technical. I imagine a chalkboard lesson. With mysteriously calculated intersecting arcs between two points—a complex web of arcs emerging from the smear of much erasure, and whose points of intersection form, themselves, a curve whose curl should tell us something. Like those crazy, curly fireworks trails emerging from collisions in a particle accelerator. Here, you see. Right here, I believe. The Quality of Interval. And look—withdrawing the blackboard to reveal another behind (Remember those?)—the curl, the Quality of Interval, essentially the same between the end of the driveway (dotted line) and the house (a childish diagram toward which we, all of us, and all disabled as the woman in the Andrew Wyeth painting, all of us are always longing).

★

I'VE RECEIVED MY NUMBER 25 RED FILTER. LITTLE PACKAGE IN THE mail. Now we shall penetrate the mysteries. I love it. Little package in the mail containing exotic possibilities. Not really so exotic to astronomy nerds, of course. But one imagines. One imagines as for accidental properties of water poured across the open end of a wooden water telescope. So, let's go over that again: "How can desire get jammed into a thing like that? Into what realm and toward what object should it seek to project itself by such a poor, unlikely instrument?"

July 20, 1:15 A.M. Well, hard to say. In the magic ruby light there may be something there. A faint suggestion. Smudgy something toward the center of the disk. I paint a washy four-inch disk with a smudgy something toward the center. Add some notes. Is this like crystal gazing? I suppose it is. That smudgy something starts to look like my reflection in John Dee's little crystal ball in the British Museum that sad, fading after-noon. Or maybe an angel. Hard to say.

July 29, 12:30 A.M. How peculiar is this. How philosophi-cally striking. Here it is, the closest approach in fifteen years and it's just dust. It all goes blank as a perfect mirror. As if one has tried too hard—held the perfumed shirt to one's face too often, summoned the buoyant, fragrant memory of Philippine mahog-any, of too many sweet, departed things too many times and now, in spite of the furtiveness, it overloads, goes dead. Can one avert one's gaze from the averting act itself and get it back? Get something back? You feel it can't be gone. Just look away again. The thing you love is still there somewhere. Just pretend you do not care for your not caring, and perhaps you catch the dear and lost and longed-for thing twice looked away from, twice refined to almost nothing, then perhaps you catch a glimpse like bril-liant motes of dust lit from behind.

*

TODAY WE VISITED, WITH FRIENDS, FOR REASONS NOT IMPORTANT here, I think, a wonderful, deteriorating nineteenth-century house in Corsicana. Though I guess I ought to mention here how we became involved in this little town about an hour south of Dallas. How the artist Doug MacWithey's widow, Karan, sold the old three-story Odd Fellows hall to a young artist friend of ours who built it into a popular artists' residency, inspiring us to purchase the "L. T. Davis—1924" grocery store across the street to make a studio for Nancy, who then sold her Dallas home and bought a small, old—1866, remodeled 1890—house an easy walk from town and on whose porch, when I've come down from Dallas, we may sit in the evenings taking in what almost passes for the past. It almost passes, I've decided, most conspicuously and sweetly right at dusk on the occasional balloon-tired bike whose rider seems so ghostly and whose weary, slow mechanics make the gentlest saddest sound out here, somehow, in the fading light. It's the out-hereness. Which, in Texas towns below a certain size—as I have noted in the case of the even smaller town of Palmer, only a few miles up the road—presents our tentative condition so explicitly. Out here we seem to have so little mass. Old houses seem to deteriorate by a kind of natural sublimation. Even history, in these lower-pressure regions, seems to evaporate, to leave a sort of haze upon the ancient ripply window glass.

Anyway, we're at this rather grand but highly sublimated old Victorian with some friends who've shown an interest. It's just come onto the market and is still furnished with that overstuffed and wildly ornamental sort of clutter you'd expect. One room is portraits—early photographic family groups and faces. Even through the frequent retouch—some entirely painted over with that strange funereal reverence for the thought above the fact—you trace resemblances. The ears, the brow. A certain stern and forthright "style" of person. All four walls. All blankly gazing in at you. Where will they go? Where have they gone?

The stained glass windows here and there are salvaged decorator pieces. All original glass is plain except, so oddly, for the front door's single pane, which is red down the center fading to pink at either side, and that of the kitchen door, which gives a uniformly deep red (number 25 red filter) view of the street. It looks like Mars out there all right. As I recall in at least one really cheap old science-fiction movie, which, for scenes on Mars, would simply drop a red gel over the lens. The glass looks old—with waves and bubbles. And a Navarro County history—from the seventies, that devotes a page to the house—notes "old red glass that permits insiders to see out but bans the vision of outsiders." Although not without a subtle inward consequence, you'd think. How old might that number 25 red filter kitchen window be? Might someone frying chicken, say, in that small, spare, high-ceilinged kitchen on a sunny day in 1900—family members looking in from time to time to take it in, that concentrated quality of hope and expectation—might she sense, out of the corner of her eye, the alien world? The Martian children, dogs, and carriages and curiously exaggerated brilliance of the clouds? Might she receive, beneath her notice, something of that same strange comfort one receives with Arcosanti's vegetarian lasagna as one gazes through those huge round windows out upon the pastness of the future?

In the corner of a small, green, tall-thin-windowed room in Nancy's Corsicana house, I have a little writing desk I found in town for fifty bucks. There's also an old iron bed; one tall and narrow and one smaller, wider bookcase; an old brass refracting astronomical telescope on a tripod; and, atop the pigeonholed hutch at the back of my desk, a six-inch globe of Mars as Percival Lowell in 1905 imagined it. Which seems to me important. Next to the five framed four-leaf clovers I discovered among the pages of a deaccessioned library book on seabirds, and below a pretty good and pretty old fake Ryder painting of a lonely fishing boat beneath the moon. This other hopeful, lonely, superstitious thing. Do you believe in Mars? I do. The way we know it ought to look—our hopes and fears drawn out upon it in those swoopy, vaguely sinister geometries. I had to make it myself. Five coats of gesso over a sanded polystyrene sphere, canals and major features lined and washed in yellow-tinted Prussian blue, with those eternal, indisputable, mythological/ancient historical names for everything in tiny India ink, all over the palest amber tint—except for the vastly expanded southern polar ice that year, left white. My friend Tim Coursey helped me make the wooden stand. The globe, with brass tube driven through, drops over a threaded rod, a little round brass finial on top. So you can spin it. Not much wobble. Just a little. It's important. Among these other things in this small green Victorian room with tall, thin windows, most with wavy, nineteenth-century glass. It is important here because, if one stands back, it reads as quaint. And in that quaintness—in that generalizing, decorating corner of the eye—the quaint, exotic thing that perfectly replaces it, stands in for it, is one of those porcelain nineteenth-century phrenological busts, so commonly reproduced, with all our hopes and fears and aptitudes and inclinations mapped and labeled over the skull's imagined corresponding regions. Look at that. They are the same.

*

JULY 30, 12:15 A.M. AM I IMAGINING THAT SMUDGINESS? THAT FAINT suggestion? Pretty much the same in any case. Diameter 24.3 arc seconds—big as it's going to get and pretty much just dust, I think. I paint a blob with an imagined smudge toward center. Wash my brush and shut it down. I see in the paper that the public is invited tomorrow night to a nearby community college campus for a telescopic viewing of Mars as well as other planets, organized by the Texas Astronomical Society. The same group that, more than sixty years ago, issued a similar invitation to that hill in Ellis County. Where I felt, somehow, the planet was descending, riding out there with my mom.

I wish I could summon, like a fragrance, something of that strange approach, that sense of driving through the dusk toward some impossible conjunction. But it's not like that, of course. It's like a trip to the hardware store. I park and follow the signs. Each person at each instrument is happy to assist you, let you have a look and answer any questions—nope, there's nothing to see right now. It's just a big orange ball of fuzz. My goodness. Yep. It's just a big orange ball of fuzz.

Yet it impinges. Wouldn't you say? I might have asked. And isn't it strange how the cicadas shriek? And how the evening light just slips away from dingy yellow into such a deep Saharan sort of redness. A resigned, nomadic redness, I would say.

We're born to lose. Like in the song. And those tattoos you used to see when such things carried more conviction. There must be a few still out there—non-ironic, fading out on fading bikers, truckers, sailors, oil-field workers. And it's true. We're preadapted in a way. Toward loss. The self itself reducing to the interval, that emptiness across which longing propagates. Those sad old rowdies know it. They can feel it in their bleeding, daggered hearts.

It's not yet midnight. Still, officially, the date of closest approach. About an hour, I would guess, before it slips behind the catalpa tree. Those telescopes out there were all set up for public use—unfiltered, modest magnification. Is there something to be gained by forcing matters? Bringing your eye right up to the knothole? Holding your breath? At 640 power you tend to hold your breath. I heave the balky shutter open—what a rough and clumsy, practical sort of noise. About as "furtive" as preparing to receive a load of hay. And what a clumsy operation altogether, for that matter, with the brush and ink. Still hoping, I suppose, for the happy accident. A poor, unlikely instrument.

I think about that rickety, weathered six-foot stepladder borrowed to support the cardboard pinhole solar telescope I built up there in Ithaca, New York, when we were visiting. What a peculiar thing to place out in the meadow. Like a scarecrow. Like a warning. Watch out. Things out here in the meadow—and this might be one—acquire, as on a Mathew Brady battlefield, a terrible simplicity. A poor old wooden stepladder made by the Babcock Ladder Company turned to such exotic duty, its remarkable collection of abraded and yet still adhering cautionary labels and instructions, use restrictions, stamps and stencils testifying as to size and suitability as if it were a rocket-engine part, does seem to gain, out here, a certain fundamental criticality. Well yes, of course, I see, now that we've set it up out here where insects chatter and the wind moves over the grass, we must be careful. There are two or three hundred words of fine instructional print—amazingly still legible. It's serious. Out here. Beyond the tedious legal exercise—a manual of comportment ("Leather soles should not be used") toward any prospect of ascent. Even to the three-foot, seven-inch maximum height advised for this particular model. Why should vertical be so hard? Long after aviation had become routine, the rocket experiments of Robert Goddard still blew up. Or shot off sideways, terrifying farmers, livestock. ("Destroy ladder if broken or worn . . .") Or worn? Defiled? It sounds rabbinical. Who knew? It is a wonder anyone finds it worth the risk. To leave the ground. Depart the horizontal prairie of the heart—for what? A coat of paint? Clean gutters? Some small insight that may prove to be both perilous and trivial? Veronica, Nancy's daughter, kindly emailed me the photos I'd neglected to take of the ladder and its labeling. She included one of Teddy and Rory climbed up on it, breaking all the rules. With Teddy perched on top, where he does not belong, and Rory halfway up and hanging off the side. They are so trivially and preciously imperiled.

July 31, still, barely. Maybe half an hour shy of the catalpa tree. At 640 power, number 25 red filter. Hold my breath. Let there be something unavailable to more responsible instruments at reasonable magnifications. I am ready. In position. Tensed and focused. There is nothing else. Just this. I'm like my daughter's little dog. Might we, like dogs, require to be loved into possession of a soul? Oh please. A good clear disk. The seeing's not too bad. But nothing. Through the ruby glass, not even a smudge. It is, in a way I guess, like 1956—that strange approach. The long drive out into the dark, that gathering sense of vast impingement. The imponderable conjunction. And then nothing. A few flashlights on the hill. The drive back home. I have a bottle of bright red ink I seldom use. A glass of water. Pour some water out, then add some ink to get the right dilution. Take the large brush and just swipe it on in big wet circular strokes right in the center of the paper. Big as a frying pan. Pink spattering, running redder here and there. Is this what Zen is like? Must be—I deeply do not care. Nor even for not caring, so removed am I at this point. So averted. Now we've got this big round empty Zen-like field of pink. Why pink? Because it's emptier than red. What can it mean? That love is distant, I suppose. That love is strange. Who knows? Just go ahead and brush the date in black. And there you go. That's it. We're done.

ACKNOWLEDGMENTS

THANKS MOST OF ALL TO NANCY, MY PARTNER IN ALL THINGS.

To my editor, Andy Ward, and my agent, Nicole Aragi, for their friendship, wisdom, and enthusiasm.

To Bonnie Thompson for her surgical yet compassionate copyediting.

And to those helping and inspiring: Anna Badkhen; Josh Bangle; Paula Bosse; Greg Cotter; Mary Cotter; John Cotton; Tim and Melanie Coursey; Charlie Drum; Vernon Grissom; Evan Horn; Courtney, Elaine, and Lila King; Paul Larson; Russell, Veronica, Theodore, and Rory Ligon; Jim Lynch; Doug MacWithey; Anthony Marks; Courtenay Paris; Barron Rector; Deborah and Joan Riddles; Kevin Schindler; Jeff Stein; Karan Verma; and Chuck Watson.

ABOUT THE TYPE

This book was set in Bembo, a typeface based on an old-style Roman face that was used for Cardinal Pietro Bembo's tract *De Aetna* in 1495. Bembo was cut by Francesco Griffo (1450–1518) in the early sixteenth century for Italian Renaissance printer and publisher Aldus Manutius (1449–1515). The Lanston Monotype Company of Philadelphia brought the well-proportioned letterforms of Bembo to the United States in the 1930s.